Skye

This book is in memory of Skye, our beloved cat, who sat by my side, keeping me company while writing this book.

August 5, 2006 – April 6, 2015
Skye
"The Professor"

CHANGE THE WORLD COOKBOOK

"A Cookbook For The Health And Welfare Of
Ourselves and All Living Creatures"

 For a moment, imagine you live on a faraway planet that does not
consume any of the other living inhabitants that you are sharing
your world with. All is peaceful. The animals have no fear.
Energy levels are high. Beautiful bountiful gardens are everywhere.
Honeybees thrive. Spirituality abounds.
You were never given meat as a child and never
imagined eating another creature.
You were brought up learning how to grow and cook your own
food made from vegetables, fruits and grains. You love all animals,
and never had a thought to harm one.
Plenty to eat, no need for meat.
And if you lived on this planet you would say, "meat? what's
meat?

This cookbook will teach you how to make healthy recipes for yourself and your
family. It's a start, a beginning, a way to slowly start making changes in our
eating habits, to bring about positive changes in our lives.
You do not need to be a Vegan or a Vegetarian to enjoy this cookbook.
If you love delicious food, then this is the cookbook for you.
This cookbook will help make the world a better place for all creatures.
(and if your are Vegan or Vegetarian you can adjust to recipes to meet your
dietary food choices)

By taking your time using baby steps, you can move forward to make smart
healthy changes in your diet and little by little, change what you eat.
Remember the ocean is but millions of drops of water.
If we all did a little at a time, like the millions of drops of water in the ocean, it
would add up to something huge and wonderful. Imagine the peaceful future we
could all share with our fellow living beings on our beautiful planet.

There are also many other ways to help, for example: by not buying fur, or not
supporting companies that use animals for experimentation, or for testing their

products. Many companies now offer products that do not use animals for testing.

This book will help provide you with ideas of how to take small steps, which will achieve positive results just by changing what you eat.

The world is full of wonderful amazing things to enjoy without harming other creatures.

Many recipes are inside, find the ones you like, make up your own, be creative and enjoy!

I hope this book becomes a lifeline for the protection of all animals, showing that people do care in trying to make the earth a better place for everyone.

So this is a cookbook for everybody to help start making healthy changes in their diets. Thus, by doing so may cause a domino effect, in helping to save the lives of animals.

"Let the dawn come. Let all the people and all the creatures have peace, let all things live happily', for the love must not only be between humans, but between all living things." (Mayan Priest/Shaman, Don Alejandro Cirilo Oxlaj Peres: "... from "The Prophecy)

And why did I write this book? It happened like this: I woke up in the middle of the night, with this idea: I have to write a cookbook for the animals. And so I did, and here it is.

I hope you enjoy this book.

(permission has been granted for all pictures, recipes and links)

Baby Steps:

Many things in our lives are accomplished with baby steps.

Not everything is accomplished with leaps and bounds.
Many things that are worth any sort of effort will take years and sometimes generations to reach a final goal.
So on with our goal of becoming more compassionate towards all life.

In dedication this book goes out to all the people who have influenced my choices in life, and the feelings I have towards my fellow inhabitants of this planet.

These people that I mention take a special place in my heart, and of course there many others not mentioned, that are my dear friends, who contributed to this cookbook. My thanks and appreciation to all of them for the time and effort they took in donating their recipes and pictures.

To my parents, Miriam and Richard Ruggles. They taught me the wonders of nature, the love of animals and the appreciation of hard work and cooking from scratch.

To Greg, the love of my life, my angel, sharing ideas and helping me try new recipes and sharing in the success of cooking, in a new and healthy way. Showing an interest in any new ideas I have, and being my recipe taster! Greg supports me with a positive attitude in all that I do, without him I would not be the free creative person that I am.

To my Sister, Jacqueline M. Sewell, my best friend and the greatest cook of all time! She does not measure, she just cooks. My sister taught me everything about cooking and making it a family occasion. She taught me the value of being together and sharing the meals she cooked. Jackie is always there providing me strength and wisdom. My sister means the world to me. I could never ever ask for more in a sister. I love her with all my heart.

To Joseph,, a wonderful son, and a man with a kind heart towards all animals. He loves nature, the outdoors and all that goes with it. He loves to cook, and he makes the best spaghetti sauce, using fresh tomatoes and chili. He is always right there when I need a helping hand. Joe has a great talent for being able to build just about anything, from building decks, shelves, skateboard ramps to building and flying helicopters.

To Naomi, another one who loves to cook. She makes the best peanut butter cookies I have ever eaten! And can cook up a storm!
I have seen her make sauce, pasta, dips and cookies all in one afternoon, and then serve a fancy dinner with all the trimmings. Amazing! Plus it's all so delicious. She is a sweetheart.

In memory of my oldest daughter, Lisa Jean, who took to heart all I taught her and added so much of her own knowledge of life, and then passed it down to her own child. A great lover of animals, always being so kind, speaking to them in such a gentle soft voice. Gathering her own eggs, from her chickens, that would walk right into her living room and eat right out of her hand.
Lisa, went on to become a great healer, and a yoga teacher, with a kind gentle soul. If I ever had any questions about health or nutrition I would call her first.

To Destiny, also a wonderful and kindhearted daughter and an awesome cook! An artist and healer with so much talent, and so smart! Destiny has an amazing green thumb, growing all kinds of vegetables. I have never seen anyone grow so much from their own garden and then turn around and make wonderful dishes from them.

To my granddaughter, Zoe Jean, a wonderful cook and a artist, so much like her mom, Lisa.
I think she got the best of everyone! talented and smart. I am sure her baby steps will carry on way into the future.
Also a protector of nature and animals. Zoe has taught me many things even now. How to buy green onions or chives and keep them growing on your windowsill. She has also introduced me to Pomegranates. A healthy wonderful new fruit I did not know about.

To Cadence, a child of my heart, a friend of Lisa's, a wonderful woman who taught me about being a Vegetarian. Growing her own herbs to make tea or for cooking. Cady, a true inspiration!

These wonderful people are my inspirations in life. My children gave me a chance to share my love of life, animals, plants, and nature with them and hopefully like baby steps it goes on for generations.

And many more wonderful friends, all amazing people that have donated many wonderful recipes that are included in this book.

CHAPTER ONE: REFLECTING

You are not alone in your struggle of not wanting to eat meat all the time. But what is one to do? Most of us are brought up eating meat since childhood, not even knowing what it is, except that it's food.
Most of the time we do not even relate meat with the animals that we are eating. It's the way we are brought up. Never really thinking about what we are eating or where it came from.

Then comes along a day when you start to realize, oh, that chicken, that you saw at the fair, or at a farm, it's chicken like what we eat. But then we brush it off, never really thinking or connecting it to the chicken we see in the supermarket.

What about pork chops, roast pork or pork fried rice? Well at least they are calling it pork, but did you connect pork to a pig as a child?
Pigs are very cool, we had two once, until we ate them. The ones we had were pink pigs, with round eyes and white eyelashes. They loved having hot grain mash for breakfast. It was my job every morning to fix it for them. They loved having their backs scratched. They were brothers, and use to sleep snuggled up together in their bed of straw.
One day when I got home from school, there they were hanging dead from a tree. Then my brother and mother made them into bacon, ham, and roasts. They were friendly pigs once and now they were our food. I did not like it when I saw that, and still do not like thinking back on how I felt seeing what happened to them.

Pigs are the smartest, cleanest domestic animals known, more so than cats and dogs, according to some experts. Some people think pigs are dirty because they like to roll in the mud, But pigs don't have sweat glands, so that is why they roll around in the mud to stay cool.

How about a cow, did you ever see one close up? They have beautiful brown eyes, long eyelashes, and soft fur. Cows are big animals, but very gentle.
The cow is the same thing as that hamburger or that steak, or the Sloppy Joe's, and tacos that we cook or buy.
Hamburger at the supermarket, wow, it does not look like that nice gentle cow.

Happy Pigs

Years go by, and you do what your use to, shopping and buying meat to make breakfast, lunch and dinner. Like, what else would I eat?

Not really thinking of where it all comes from and not trying to make other choices for food. But sometimes you do think about it, maybe when you read an article on the way meat is processed, or you hear of an outbreak of some foodborne disease. Or you might see pictures of a slaughterhouse, and notice how the animals are treated and are Mass Produced like objects. The fact is that thousands and thousands of animals are killed and processed each day by the food companies. The animals feeling are never taken into consideration.

This is a fact you can look up:
In the USA 23 million chickens are killed every day,
100,000 cows (4000 every hour) and
112 million pigs are killed every year.
And probably these figures are growing every day.

http://www.upc-online.org/slaughter/2000...
http://www.da4a.org/food.htm

Does it bother you? But stopping it all seems impossible.
And then off shopping we go, and the counters are full of meat. So much meat, and it's so easy to buy, and we forget again. Or we think of a favorite recipe like meatloaf, or stuffed cabbage and we forget and buy meat. I know I did it all the time.
 But then one day I heard someone say, we can make changes little by little, fork by fork. So by eating less meat, it will affect the market, and how much is produced by the meat companies. They work on supply and demand. So even if we think we are not making a dent, we are. Little by little, a change here and there and before you know it we are making a difference.

Every time I would shop and buy meat it would bother me. So I would make excuses, it taste's so good, it's good for us, or my husband likes his steak, or my kid's love their burgers. So I would stock up on meat products, not really realizing the terrible torture these creatures endure so we can eat them.
Sometimes I don't even think it's the meat we like so much, but it's the things we put on the meat that make us like it so much.
Garlic, onions, mushrooms, ketchup, relish, mustard, and horseradish. Yum! These are not meat, but we love the taste of these products.
I will help show you how to make changes, and its not that hard to do.

My sister told me how she loves to butter a hot dog roll, pan toast it and put relish, mustard and ketchup on it, with no hot dog, it's so good just like that.

And there is so much food today to choose from. Way back in the olden days people did depend on hunting for food, and raising animals to feed their families, but all that has changed. Look at how many kinds of food are available today in our supermarkets besides meat that is also healthy for us.
So today we do have options to eat healthy, wise, and cruelty free.

Some people find it easy to do this change in little steps. The first step to take is, say, for example, the choice of not eating red meat anymore. Once you adjust to that, you could then stop eating pork. We adjust and move on. This is a good way to filter out things in our life that we want to change. And once in a while you might eat it, but a big change has been made when you make these choices. Besides that, you will feel good about the changes you have made.

That is why I wrote this book, from a person who feels its wrong to harm these wonderful animals, who are soft and gentle, with beautiful eyes, that will look back into ours, with emotions and feelings. These animals also have their own lives to live. Don't forget that we were brought up reading storybooks about all the wonderful animals. Do you remember how much you loved to go to a zoo or a farm and see them? When we looked at and admired these animals, we were not looking at them and thinking of how good they were going to look or taste on our plates!

We don't eat our pets, so why eat the wild creatures or the farm animals? They are the same. Earth must be terrible for animals raised for food. I will not go into it in this book, but do some research on the methods the slaughterhouses use, and see for yourself. Check out the You Tube video that Paul McCartney documented: "If Slaughterhouses Had Glass Walls Everyone Would Be A Vegetarian," He did a wonderful job on this video, it's one everyone should see and then decide for themselves. And if you start to lose your determination, watch the video again. Our hearts are kind, so if we were shown what was done, like this video does, it would have a great effect on us. Some people say," oh, I cannot watch this, its too sad." Yes it is, but we need to see these things and be educated on what is going on. We need to teach our children and future generations what is right and wrong.

One thing that bothers me, is that it seems to me, that the companies that produce meat, do not seem to care about the animal's own lives or happiness. Do you think that their main concern is feeding people, and that it's important to supply food? Or do you think it's the profit margins?
I think the real reason they are in business is that they are thinking of ways to

make money and how to make more and more money, faster and faster.

They are Mass Producing animals in warehouses to make a profit. Most animals never see the light of day their whole lives. Imagine that! Being born and never seeing the sun, or being outside. The meat companies are not thinking of the welfare of the animals. Again, please do some research on the life of these animals.

And, do you think by forcing an animal to die against its will, is right? I have never seen a animal volunteer to die. They always run. Basically they are afraid of humans. It's a smart instinct for them to have.

I am trying to list options on ways to eat to reduce the amount of meat in your diet.

Follow it everyday, or some days, or a few days per week.

Eat less meat and maybe someday you won't eat any.

For each person that becomes a Vegetarian about 100 animals are not needed. After 10 years that's 1000 animals, so if you were a vegetarian for 50 years you saved about 5000 animals.

I am sure you can think of many things to eat that are not meat. Make your own list and see. Some people choose to not eat meat, fish, or seafood and some don't use any animal products at all. Some don't use eggs. It's all up to you.

But take one step at a time and move at your own pace. It's your journey.

You can do it, and it might take time, or you might make the changes right away, it's all up to you.

Think of all the years you have been eating animals, you have a habit, and it's a hard habit to break. So don't feel guilty, be proud you are taking steps to change things.

So if you can do this, even at a slow pace, you will have a clear conscience and become healthier, feel better and just feel good about yourself.

Then go visit some animals and see how wonderful they really are.

No one should suffer to feed another. Sharing our meals, or having a nice dinner should be a happy experience for everyone, right?

So when we sit around the dinner table with our families, laughing and talking and being so joyful, how can we be happy if we understood the suffering that some of our food might have gone through?

Humans are not the only ones who should be feel happy, we are all here to enjoy the earth we share.

Learning to love and respect all creatures is important to our own self-esteem and growth as a human race.

This can be accomplished by taking little steps to reach our personal goal of changing our eating habits to a more healthy and compassionate way.

I did not do this all at once either. So, for example, on my first day of shopping I walked right by the meat counter, which surprisingly gave me such a feeling of freedom!

It's hard to explain, but it felt really good. Imagine just walking by the meat counter and not having to purchase any of it!

So I chose to not eat any meat except for occasional seafood as a beginning. My first shopping order consisted of buying eggplant, to make homemade Eggplant Parmesan. Some salad greens, radish, scallions, tomatoes, cucumbers, and peppers for healthy salads.

I also bought, the ingredients to make Spinach Calzones. I use mushrooms, vegan cheese and onions. I also bought pasta to make American Chop Suey, eggs, beansprouts, and mushrooms for Egg Foo Yong. Did you know that beansprouts contains all the healthy nutrients you need?

I also bought what I needed to make Chili. Last week I made Chili and it was gone in a flash. No one even noticed there was no meat in it. The Textured Vegetable Protein is just like hamburger and its great for sauces and Chili. Anything that calls for ground hamburger can be substituted with the Textured Vegetable Protein. I also purchased fresh vegetables, broccoli, yams, potatoes, peppers and Jalapeno Peppers.

So what did I make for supper? Boiled potatoes, which I served with "Earth Balance" a butter spread substitute, salt and pepper. Fried onions with garlic, peppers and scallions, and fresh buttered broccoli and baked fish. Not a bad meal for a beginner.

Don't forget, you don't have to go cold turkey! You can start off by eating less meat products.

So on to the recipes. Enjoy and good health to you, to great food, and happiness to all creatures great and small. Get creative and add some of your own ideas. One bit of advice, if you are the main cook in your family, you don't have to even tell them, that you are eating less meat, just cook great meals and they might not even miss it. You can slowly make the switch and keep everyone happy..

A happy rabbit by Zoe Jean Kingsley

CHAPTER TWO: EGGS

Eggs from our very own chickens

Some people do not eat eggs and say it is wrong to eat them. I personally do not think its wrong to eat eggs, if you can purchase them from chickens that are not factory farmed. We have our own chickens, and they lay fresh eggs everyday. The chickens do not want their eggs, they lay them and walk away and that is it. The only time a chicken wants the eggs it lays is when it wants to hatch baby chicks. We do not have any roosters, so no rooster, no baby chicks.

As long as the chickens are happy I think using eggs are fine, so buying cage free eggs is an option you should check out. The best place to get eggs is at a local farmer.

Do some research on how factory chickens are kept in small cages their whole lives, never leaving the cage until they are too old to lay eggs, and where do they go when they are too old?

Off to the slaughterhouse they go. Like thanks for the eggs, now its time to die, after a terrible life, of not moving, toes growing into the wire cages, having their bills cut off, no sunshine, nothing buy misery. These are the way eggs are Mass Produced.

So make sure you buy cage free eggs, and find out what companies really have true cage free chickens. What they cost more? What is a dollar or two more? So what! Or better yet, go to a farm if you have any near you then you can buy fresh eggs. Nothing tastes better than a farm fresh egg. Some say the cage free chickens do not have a much better life, as they are over crowded too, so farm fresh eggs are the best choice. You could also get a few laying hens for yourself, for fresh eggs and they also make good pets.

a typical hen house that is cage free.

Here is some information on cage produced eggs:

Battery Cages

The vast majority of egg-laying hens in the United States are confined in battery cages. On average, each caged laying hen is afforded only 67 square inches of cage space—less space than a single sheet of letter-sized paper on which to live her entire life. Unable even to spread their wings, caged laying hens are among the most intensively confined animals.

Caged hens also suffer from the denial of many natural behaviors such as nesting, perching, and dust bathing, all are important activities for a hen's welfare. Numerous scientists have spoken clearly about the animal welfare problems with battery cages. One such scientist, Nobel Prize winner Dr. Konrad Lorenz, said:

"The worst torture to which a battery hen is exposed is the inability to retire somewhere for the laying act. For the person who knows something about animals it is truly heart-rending to watch how a chicken tries again and again to crawl beneath her fellow cage mates to search there in vain for cover."

Cage-Free Systems

Because of public opposition to battery cage confinement, many egg producers are switching to cage-free systems. These systems generally offer hens a significantly improved level of animal welfare than do battery cage systems, though the mere absence of cages sometime isn't enough to ensure high welfare.

Unlike battery hens, cage-free hens are able to walk, spread their wings and lay their eggs in nests, vital natural behaviors denied to hens confined in cages. Most cage-free hens live in very large flocks that can consist of many thousands of hens who never go outside. The vast majority of cage-free hens live on farms that are 3rd-party audited by certification programs that mandate perching and dust-bathing areas. These advantages are very significant to the animals involved. Dr. Michael Appleby, one of the world's leading poultry welfare experts:

"Battery cages present inherent animal welfare problems, most notably by their small size and barren conditions. Hens are unable to engage in many of their natural behaviors and endure high levels of stress and frustration. Cage-free egg production, while not perfect, does not entail such inherent animal welfare disadvantages and is a very good step in the right direction for the egg industry."

Cage-free hens are spared several severe cruelties that are inherent to battery cage systems. But it would nevertheless be a mistake to consider cage-free facilities to necessarily be "cruelty-free." Here are some of the more typical sources of animal suffering associated with both types of egg production:

- Both systems typically buy their hens from hatcheries that kill the male chicks upon hatching—more than 200 million each year in the United States alone.

- Both cage and cage-free hens have part of their beaks burned off, a painful mutilation.

- Both cage and cage-free hens are typically slaughtered at less than two years old, far less than half their normal lifespan. They are often transported long distances to slaughter plants with no food or water.

- While the vast majority of the battery and cage-free egg industry no longer uses starvation to force molt the birds, there are battery and cage-free producers alike who still use this practice.

So, while cage-free does not necessarily mean cruelty-free, cage-free hens generally have significantly better lives than those confined in battery cages. The ability to lay their eggs in nests, run and spread their wings are tangible benefits that shouldn't be underestimated.

(www.humansociety.org)

Luna Eclipse, one of our fancy pet chickens

We have 6 hens and our yard is fenced in so they can roam free. They love to lay in the sun to take a nap. Chickens can recognize each other and have social levels. They are all friends with each other. They go to bed before dark because they are afraid something will kill them. So at dusk they all head back to the chicken coop, and jump up inside and cuddle close together. Then I go out and lock the doors until morning to protect them from predators.

One day I was watching them, and a hawk flew into a nearby tree. All the chickens ran and hid in the shed or under the pine trees. That made me realize, that they are afraid and do not want to die. They did not stand out bravely and say " oh, kill me and eat me for food, hawk, I am tasty, here I am!" So they are worried about their lives, just like we would be or any other creature. They do not want to get eaten.

Eggs are healthy for you. Eggs contain lots of protein. And they do not raise your cholesterol. Years ago the heart association took eggs off of many people's diets, saying they were bad. Today they say you can eat them. So, if your worried about your fat intake, stop eating so much junk food. It's loaded with bad fats.
So, for myself, I would rather eat eggs for protein, then take the life of an animal. Taking eggs from a chicken does not hurt the chicken.

Here is some information on eggs, and then we will get to some good cooking ideas.

Eggs are a great source of protein. Numerous vitamins, including vitamin A, potassium and many B vitamins like folic acid, choline and biotin, are also packed into this oval-shaped staple [Source: USDA]. In fact, very few foods share the same diverse nutrient makeup available in a single egg. Many of these are specifically needed for the health of the nerves and the brain. Through the years, all fats have become public enemies, often blamed for an increased risk of heart disease. Eggs fell out of favor and people gravitated toward egg whites as a substitute. In truth, the yolk is where many of the vitamins and nutrients are found.

The topic of cholesterol has become very confusing. Dietary advice on the subject is often so far off that consumers actually hurt their health by trying to avoid cholesterol. The body needs to achieve a balance when it comes to cholesterol consumption. Fat from healthy sources is vital to the body, while fat from poor choices, such as margarine or foods fried in vegetable oil, are very dangerous. Eggs remain a beneficial source of healthy fat. Many nutrients, such as vitamin A, are better absorbed with fat, making eggs a very good source of vitamin A. Research has documented that eggs do not appear to promote heart disease risk [Source: Kritchevsky, Djousse].

Diabetics may be one of the only groups that should avoid averaging more than one egg a day, as they might show some increases in cholesterol with higher egg consumption. But even in diabetics, eggs can be very helpful. Much of the standard breakfast for Americans is laden with sugar. Waffles, pancakes, pastries, gourmet coffees and most breakfast cereals offer little or no nutritional value and are often loaded with sugar. These foods are poor choices for diabetics, and the rest of us.

HARD BOILED EGGS:
What could be any easier?
Boil up a dozen eggs. Cool and put in the refrigerator. Peel and eat with a little salt and pepper.

Hard Boiled Eggs

Place eggs in saucepan large enough to hold them in single layer. Add cold water to cover eggs by 1 inch. Heat over high heat just to boiling. Remove from burner. cover the pan.
Let eggs stand in hot water about 12 minutes for large eggs (9 minutes for medium eggs; 15 minutes for extra large).

Drain immediately and serve warm or cool completely under cold running water or in bowl of ice water, then refrigerate

STUFFED EGGS:

Take your hard boiled eggs, and peel. For each egg you peel, you will be able to make two stuffed eggs.
Once you peel enough eggs, take a thin knife and cut them in half the long way.
Scoop out the yellow centers into a little bowl. Place the half's you cut on a plate, as you will be filling these with the yellow egg centers that we prepare.

Mash the yellow centers, and add enough mayo to make it moist. Salt and pepper to taste.
Now fill the little empty center of the white half, and then sprinkle the tops with parsley or paprika.
Keep cold until you serve them.
These make great snacks for kids too.

Eggs For breakfast or anytime of the day.

Think of all the things you can make with eggs.

SCRAMBLED EGGS:

Crack two or three eggs into a bowl. Add a little soy milk, salt and pepper and whip with a fork until well mixed.
Heat your frying pan, use some olive oil or spray with cooking oil, and Pour in your eggs. Stir and cook until done.

Now you can prepare some things that can be added to your eggs. Here are some suggestions:

Mushrooms, peppers, onions, jalapeno peppers, scallions, cheese, spinach, garlic, or asparagus.

Just cook them in your pan and when they are done, pour in the eggs and scramble. Or you can precook the items and add them when you cook the eggs.

Scrambled eggs can also be put on toast, or English muffins or bagels to make a scrambled egg sandwich.

EGGS ON TOAST:

First of all the pan is important when you make eggs on toast. I like a deep little saucepan, and you will also need a strainer ladle to scoop out the eggs from the water.

Fill the pan to about ½ inch from the top, salt the water and bring it to a boil. Then turn down the heat, as you don't want too heavy a boil, as it will mess up your eggs.
Then crack two eggs and drop them gently into the water. Bring up the heat again to a gentle boil.
Pop two slices of toast into the toaster. Usually the time it takes the toast to cook is about the time it takes the eggs to be ready. You can stick a fork into the whites to see if they are done enough for you.
When done, life the eggs out with the strainer and drain off the water.
Place them on your buttered toast, salt and pepper and your done.
These make great meals. We have them for supper many nights.

Pan Fried Eggs

FRIED EGGS:

Use a frying pan, put in a couple pats of Earth Balance, or use pam
or olive oil and when the pan is nice and hot, crack open a couple of
eggs and gently put them in the pan and cook. Flip them over when
the whites looks cooked enough to do so.

Fried eggs are great with home fried potatoes, potato cakes, fish
cakes, or fried yams.
I really like fried eggs on top of a dish of home fried potatoes

Home Fried Potatoes:

You can use regular potatoes but yams are good too.
You do not need to peel the potatoes, but I do peel the yams.
Cut the potatoes up into small squares. Place oil in your frying

pan, heat and add the potatoes. Salt and pepper, and cook and stir until tender. Sometimes it's good to add a chopped onion and minced garlic for extra flavor.

If you like them spicy you can add a few chopped jalapeno peppers. You can also use boiled potatoes to just make sure they are cold before you cut them up.

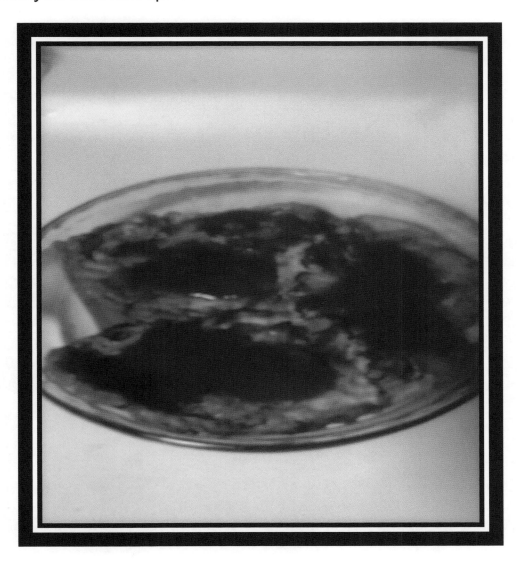

Egg Foo Young

EGG FOO YOUNG:

This is a great dish, for breakfast, lunch or dinner. You can make a stack of them and reheat them as needed. Use gravy for a topping or none at all. The choice is yours.

What you need to do is this:

Crack open 8 eggs and put in a bowl. Add one bag of fresh bean spouts. (12 ounces)
Add chopped onion, scallions, chopped peppers, canned mushrooms, salt and pepper.

You can put in whatever you like.
Mix well. Do not add milk or any other liquids.

Heat oil in your frying pan. When the oil is hot, use a ladle and scoop out the egg mixture and place a ladle full in the pan. Cook until browned and flip it over.
Press down the center to make sure the center is cooked.
Top with gravy. Makes about 6-8

I am sure if you look in a cookbook you will find many other recipes for eggs.

Some more little tidbits about eggs:

Low in calories, high in vitamins (D, B12, folic acid), and nearly perfect in protein. An egg contains every single vitamin (except C).
When eggs are digested they produce proteins that mimic the action of powerful blood pressure-lowering drugs, known as Ace inhibitors.

A recent Surrey University study found eating one or two eggs for breakfast could help with weight loss as the high protein content makes us feel fuller longer.

CHAPTER THREE: BREAKFAST OPTIONS

There are many options for breakfast Oatmeal is a good old standby.
Try adding your favorite fruit.
You can increase the health benefits of oatmeal by adding
Flax Seed, Chia Seed or Hemp Seed.
(purchase these items at your local health food store. Read the
package, to learn what great health benefits they contain)

Dried or frozen fruits, such as apricots, prunes, raisins, bananas, Strawberries and blueberries make great additions to any cereal.

Granola is good too. Granola's are high in sugar but hits the spot for a quick snack or in a bowl with a little soy, coconut, flax or almond milk.

Switching over from dairy to other options is good for your health and better for the cows. Did you realize that dairy farms artificially pregnate the cows so they produce milk? They keep the cow in a state of pregnancy so they keep producing milk.

This is unnatural. Once the calf is born it is taken away from its mother, to be raised as another dairy cow or slaughtered for veal. Did you know that veal is a baby cow? Most baby male cows are slaughtered to make veal.

Mother cows are very upset when the baby is taken away. They moo for weeks for the lost baby. Did you know, that if you separate mother cows from their babies and reunite them weeks later, they know each other and who's baby is theirs or not.

Other Breakfast Food Options:

Muffins, danish, toast, bagels, donuts and dry prepared cereals.
These are not great foods to eat, as they contain white flour, sugar
and unhealthy fats.
Use them are an option and are nice for an occasional treat.

QI'A SUPERFOOD,
It's Chia, Buckwheat, and Hemp cereal, with cranberry and vanilla.
You only need two tablespoons for a serving and you can add
coconut or soy or almond milk.
Its awesome and wicked healthy and organic.

Other options are soy and coconut milk yogurt. You can add many
items to yogurt such as fruits and seeds.
These are good tasty options to help us
eliminate the dairy we are using and besides,its more healthy for us.
Dairy products are basically all fat.

Vegetable Protein Shakes make a great meal. They also provide you with plenty of protein, vitamins and minerals.

If you would like to lose some weight, then replace a meal each day with a shake. If this does not work for you, have a shake for breakfast and lunch, then have a healthy dinner. Drink plenty of water. Eat a apple each day and have a hard boiled egg between the shakes. Also eating eight almonds each day to provide the essential oils you need.

The way I like to make my shake:

In a blender pour in one glass of almond or coconut milk, add 1 scoop of protein shake, 4 ice cubes and blend until the ice has melted. It will come out like a thick frappe. This also makes a healthy choice for a snack at night instead of eating chips or ice creams while watching your favorite shows.

You can add any fruit or vegetable you like to the shake. It's amazing how good they taste.

One shake I recommend to use is: Plant-Based Vega One (all-in-one) nutritional shake.

Waffles, french toast, pancakes, crepes, toaster strudel, pop tarts, hot cereals, Ezekiel 4:9 brand bread toasted with peanut butter, or almond butter.

.

Almond Butter is great just as a snack. Try eating almond butter plain. I will have a teaspoon as a snack to hold me over. It's also a good snack between shakes.
There are so many good things to eat that are not meat.

Use your imagination. Dinner leftovers also make a good breakfast. Remember foods that you buy, that are already prepared, such as pop tarts, dry cereal, and toaster strudel are not as healthy as cooking fresh food yourself.

If you are looking to eat healthy, one of the best breads to buy is Ezekiel 4:9 Sprouted Wheat. They have raisin, sesame seed and plain wheat.
This type of bread does not raise your blood sugar and are actually a meal in itself. You will be amazed when you read the label.
Some grocery stores are stocking this brand, if not ask them to get it. Or you can usually get it in your local health food store.
Ezekiel also makes English muffins, which are also healthy and wholesome.

Ezekiel Bread is great toasted with jam, or just plain with Earth Balance.
It makes a great grilled cheese sandwich. I find it better toasted when making sandwiches rather then not toasted.
You can keep it frozen and use as needed.

Another great option for bread is pita bread. Joseph's Flax Oat brand. It has no trans fats, reduced carb and reduced fat and is high in protein and low in carbs.

This is tasty toasted or as a sandwich, or topped with peanut butter.

CHAPTER FOUR: PET FOOD

VEGETARIAN DOG FOOD:

Many people have eliminated meat from their diet but are afraid to do so with their beloved pet because they believe that dogs are meant to be carnivores. But many dogs do quite well on a vegan diet.

There are several brands of vegan kibble on the market Nature's Balance, V-dog, Wenaewe, Pet Guard, Avo Derm, Natural Life, Evolution Diet and Wysong but you can also make your own.

To make your own: cook brown rice, storing leftovers in your fridge. Do the same with a bag of beans and steam or bake sweet potatoes. Every day put brown rice, beans and either a sweet potato or thawed frozen peas into their bowl. You can also mix in a cooked egg. You can also add chopped fresh apples and zucchini and green beans.

Sam

Dogs are also fond of fond of: corn, peas, sweet potatoes, black beans, kidney beans, black soy beans, tempeh, apples, bananas, carrots, cucumbers, zucchini, asparagus, brown rice, collard greens, kale, spinach, whole grain cereal and oatmeal and canned pumpkin and flax seed oil is important. You can add a few drops to each meal.

Brown rice is preferred over white rice as it has more nutrients and more fiber. White rice is stripped of its outer , which contains all of the good nutrients.

Using a combination of the foods above would give your dog a variety and a good source of nutrients.You can also use aveg-e-dog supplement as a proactive measure, or a vitamin supplement for dogs.

SOME SUGGESTED RECIPES:

Homemade Sweet-Potato Peanut-Butter Vegan-Dog Delight: Mix 6 cups (filtered) water, 1 cup mixed rice and quinoa (I mix black, brown, and long grain rice with black and/or white quinoa.)1 cup mixed lentils (I mix green, red, and French lentils.)3 medium sweet potatoes sliced into 1-inch cubes3 cups or 24 oz. natural peanut butter1½ cups or 8 to 12-oz. apple cider vinegar, optional (If you dog gets gassy use the vinegar, if not omit the vinegar) 1 Tbsp hemp protein,1 Tbsp. flaxseed oil with DHA (Store in the fridge or freezer.) 200-250 mg cranberry extract (Since a vegan diet is alkalizing, your dog may need this acidifier to maintain a healthy urinary pH.) VegeDog multivitamin powder Prozyme Plus (This helps with digestion so that your dog can absorb as many nutrients as possible.)125 mg PB8 brand probiotic (1/4 pill)

Boil the water.

Add the rice, lentils, and sweet potatoes.

Reduce the heat and simmer, covered, for 40 minutes to 1 hour, or until all ingredients are soft. Stir occasionally and add more water as needed. Too much water is better than not enough water. (Remember, you want the ingredients to be extra moist because they will be easier to digest.)

Mash the sweet potatoes with a fork and mix thoroughly. Let cool.

Add the peanut butter and vinegar. Stir well.

Place 3 to 5 servings in your refrigerator and store the rest in the freezer.

Measure 2/3 cup of food per meal.*

At mealtime: Add hemp protein, flaxseed oil, cranberry extract, Vegedog, Prozyme Plus, and PB8 into the 2/3 cup of food. Mix well and serve twice daily.

* Serving size is based on the diet of a 20-lb. dog. Please adjust the portion size to suit your dog's weight.

Note: Please remember, as with the introduction of any new food, to introduce this new diet gradually. This means replacing a small portion of your dog's current food with the new food and gradually increasing the amount of new food while decreasing the amount of old food over a period of approximately 10 days.

Puppy

VEGAN DOG TREATS:

- 9 cups whole wheat flour
- 1 cup nutritional yeast1 Tbsp. salt
- 1 Tbsp. garlic powder

Mix dry ingredients. Add approximately 3 cups water. Knead into a pliable dough. Roll out to 1/8" thickness. Cut into desired shapes.Bake for 10-15 minutes at 350°F. (Important: After turning off oven, leave biscuits in the oven overnight or for an 8-hour period so they become hard and crunchy.

DOG BONES;

- 3 cups minced parsley
- 1/4 cup carrots, chopped very fine
- 2 tablespoons olive oil
- 2 3/4 cups whole wheat flour
- 2 tablespoons bran
- 2 teaspoons baking powder
- 1/2 to 1 cup of water

Directions

Preheat oven to 350 degrees, rack on middle level. Lightly grease a large baking sheet.

Stir together parsley, carrots and oil. combine all the dry ingredients and add to veggies. Gradually add 1/2 cup of water, mixing well. Make a moist but not wet dough. If needed, add a little more water. Knead for one minute.

Roll dough out to 1/2 inch thickness. Using cookie cutter or a glass, cut out the shapes and transfer them to the baking sheet. Gather the scraps and reroll and cut.

Bake for 20–30 minutes until biscuits have browned and hardened slightly. (They will harden more as they cool.) Speed cooling by placing them on wire racks. Store in airtight tin.

Rufus

Want to make homemade, healthy, inexpensive meals for your pets? With VegeDog Supplements you can. These products come with healthy recipes which show you how to make your own homemade cat food or homemade dog food. Many of the ingredients in the recipes can be bought in the bulk section of a health food store. Preparing your own pet food is healthy for pets and also less expensive in the long run: check out more on these at: petvegetarianfood.com

Charlie

Dog Food recipe :

(1/2 batch Garbanzo & Soy and 1/2 batch Oat and Soy)
7 1/2 c garbanzo beans, home cooked, drained & cooled
9 1/4 c cooked, cooled rolled oats
1 2/3 c tofu, drained & mashed
3 3/4 Tbsp. oil, high oleic safflower, sunflower, or olive oil
2 Tbsp. t. yeast powder
1 Tbsp. + 1 1/2 tsp. Vegedog
1 1/2 tsp. (1/2 Tbsp.) Bragg Liquid Aminos, or 1/4 tsp salt (omit salt if using canned beans)
Mash cooked garbanzo beans (I pour into my food processor as it is running). Add cooked, cooled oats and mashed tofu. Mix well. Add remaining ingredients and stir until well blended. Store in the refrigerator. Can be frozen. Makes 4 qts. You can add 4 or 5 cups of cooked mashed green peas to this batch of food if you like. Dogs love peas and they are a great source of protein.

Blueberry

NOTES for cat food: Cats should always be slowly acclimated to new food if possible. Adoptees can't be, of course. Cats MUST have tofu that is made without magnesium chloride or Nigari. Theses are the only brands to get, Silken Mori Nu and Cost Co carries a three pack of hard style organic tofu.

Skye and Simba

Cat Food recipe
(1 batch Chickpea Plus and 1/2 batch Oats Plus from Vegecat recipes)

1 1/2 c chick peas, home cooked, drained & cooled
1 1/2 c cooked, cooled rolled oats
1 c Mori Nu silken tofu or the CostCo hard style, drained and mashed
(or you can also use plain tempeh or soaked and cooked soybeans
from dry)
(NOTE: Make sure the tofu doesn't have magnesium chloride!)
1/4 c + 2 Tbsp. Vege Yeast powder
2 Tbsp. + 1/2 .tsp. Vegecat phi
1 Tbsp. + 2 tsp. oil, high oleic safflower or sunflower, or olive oil
If you plan to freeze the food, don't add the oil until feeding
time. You'll have to figure out how much to add at each feeding)
1 tsp. Bragg Liquid Aminos, or 1/8 heaping tsp salt

Mash cooked, cooled chick peas (pour into a food processor as it is

running). Add cooked, cooled oats and mashed tofu and mix well by hand. Add remaining ingredients and stir until well blended. Store in an airtight container in the refrigerator. Can be frozen.
Makes 1 qt.

This is a site that you can purchase already prepared vegan food for both cats and dogs.

VEGANCATS.COM

Baby

Here is a example of one of the cat foods they carry. They also have dog food.

Evolution Cat Kibble is formulated to meet the nutritional levels established by the AAFCO cat food nutrient profiles for all life stages from kitten to adult. Manufactured by a vegan owned company that makes exclusively vegan pet foods (no meat products in anything they make!), this formula contains whole grains, vegetable proteins, vegetable oil, herbs, vitamins and minerals (and Taurine, too!) This way you can feed cats a diet that's cruelty-free and avoid unhealthy preservatives, slaughterhouse waste, saturated animal fats, antibiotic residues and artificial colors and flavors. Regular meat-based cat food is comprised of the lowest-grade leftovers from the meat industry and can be comprised of many things you'd never willingly want your companion animals to eat, so by feeding them Evolution food you know you're only getting healthy natural vegetable-based ingredients and not the waste that's unfit for human (and likely animal) consumption. Just like people you can make a slow switch by giving them less meat and more healthy options.

Amazon.com also lists vegan cat and dog food.

Sylvester

CHAPTER FIVE: TEXTURED VEGETABLE PROTEIN

From "wiki"

Textured or **texturized vegetable protein (TVP)**, also known as **textured soy protein (TSP)**, **soy meat**, or **soya chunks** is a defatted soy flour product, a by-product of extracting soybean oil.[1] It is often used as a meat analogue or meat extender. It is quick to cook, with a protein content equal to that of meat.

Textured vegetable protein is a versatile substance; different forms allow it to take on the texture of whatever ground meat it is substituting.

Using TVP, one can make vegetarian or vegan versions of traditional meat dishes, such as chili con carne, spaghetti bolognese, sloppy joes, tacos, burgers, or burritos.

Textured vegetable protein can be found in natural food stores and larger supermarkets, usually in the bulk section. TVP is also very lightweight and is often used in backpacking recipes. Because of its relatively low cost, high protein content, and long shelf life, TVP is often used in prisons and schools, as well as for disaster preparedness

This is a wonderful product, as it is so much like ground hamburger.

Some Tips:

When I measure out the amount to use, two cups will be a good size for a recipe equal to a pound of hamburger.
Put two cups in a bowl and add 12 ounces of vegetable soup stock.
Once the liquid is absorbed it will be light in color. If you would like it darker add some gravy master. Sometimes I add a little soy sauce.

Another method, which I think tastes better, is to fry your onions and garlic, salt and pepper, add the textured vegetable protein and cook and stir, add enough liquid until the desired texture is achieved.

The vegetable protein will take up the flavor that you add to it.
The price is usually about 3.99 per pound, but its light, so you are getting a good value, as only two cups will double in size.

If you cannot buy this at a local health food store you can purchase it online.. For example you can buy it on Amazon, and I am sure many other places have it.

Chili

AWESOME CHILI:

Chili is a great recipe that you can adjust to your own taste, and add different foods that you like to the recipe.
It's fun to experiment.
I am going to give you a general recipe that I like.
Some people use their own spices, but I usually buy a premixed chili spice.

Buy a chili mix, I found a brand called: Stonemill Essentials, which I really like and Mccormick makes one called Smokey BBQ that has a great flavor. I also found another one by Mccormick, that is called White Chili and you could substitute the chicken with tofu.

But you can find all kinds in the grocery store or you can use your own spices. Such as chili pepper, onion salt, garlic salt, curry, cumin, turmeric. Use all or use just the ones you like.

First mix two cups of vegetable protein, with the vegetable stock. While it's absorbing the liquids you can prepare the other items.
Cut up two onions, and a few fresh garlic toes and start browning them in olive oil.
Sometimes after it has browned up, I add some fresh chopped tomatoes and I also like to add fresh chopped jalapeno peppers.

If you don't want to use the vegetable protein you can fry a package of chopped mushrooms with a chopped onion and some garlic toes sliced. Once this is done, follow the rest of the directions for chili.

We grew the jalapeno peppers in our garden and you should try it. They are easy to grow. Buy a few plants at your local nursery and plant them, water them and they will produce plenty of peppers. I have even grown them in containers on our deck.
To prepare jalapeno peppers, you would use about six. You will need to slice them in half and remove the seeds. (if you want it extra hot, leave in the seeds)
I remove all the seeds and slice the peppers and add them to the onions.

Cook and stir that for about five minutes.
Now you can add your seasonings or chili mix.
Also add the vegetable protein.

This can all now be poured into a big saucepan.
Add 2 cans (8 0z. each) of tomato sauce
1 can (14 0z) diced tomatoes or you can use the whole tomatoes, just chop them up first and use the juice too.
Add 2 or 3 cans of beans, whatever kind you like. Kidney, or Great Northern Beans etc. Sometimes I will add a jar of Marianna sauce and a small can of corn and a small can of green beans.

Bring this mixture to a boil, stir and turn the heat down and simmer ten minutes.
Top with grated cheese, sour cream or chopped scallion if desired.

American Chop Suey

AMERICAN CHOP SUEY:

Buy one box of elbow macaroni.
Follow directions on box and cook the whole box.
Drain and butter lightly.

You will need to prepare two cups of vegetable protein with the
Vegetable stock described before.

In a frying pan sauté one chopped onion and one green pepper,
diced. Once they are cooked add two cans of tomato soup.
Stir and cook a few minutes.
Add the Vegetable Protein, stir and mix until hot and coated with the
sauce.
Then mix sauce with the elbows.

Serve with Italian bread and a salad.

SLOPPY JOES:

You can make Sloppy Joe's with the Textured Vegetable Protein. Follow the
directions on the Sloppy Joe canned sauce. Instead of hamburger use your Vegetable Protein.
One pound of meat is usually required so use two cups of Vegetable Protein and one can of stock to moisten. Then mix with the sauce and heat.
Serve on soft rolls.

SPAGHETTI SAUCE:

Make your favorite sauce. For meat make the Vegetable Protein as we explained. Add it to your sauce.
I like to slice in a box of fresh mushrooms as I cook my sauce
Simmer until done.

You can now use your sauce for making Lasagna, or
Ravioli. It's also a great topping to put on Spaghetti Squash.
This sauce is delicious by itself in a bowl topped with grated cheese.

Did you ever try baked spaghetti?

Make your pasta, set aside. Oil the bottom of a large baking dish, and put some sauce on the bottom. Put in your pasta, and cover with your sauce. Then top it off with shredded cheese.
Cover and bake 350 degrees until cheese is melted.

Hamburg Sundae

HAMBURG SUNDAE: (without meat)

Make a dish of mashed potatoes. You can use instant or make homemade mashed potatoes. It's your choice.

Prepare two cups of Vegetable Protein using stock to moisten.

Put some olive oil in a frying pan, add a cup of chopped onion, one diced green pepper, and a couple cloves of garlic, chopped. Salt and pepper to taste. Cook until done.
Add the Vegetable Protein and two tablespoons of Gravy Master and cook until hot. Thicken if needed with cornstarch
Serve on top of your mashed potatoes.

Shepard's Pie

SHEPARD'S PIE:

Make the same filling you did for the recipe above.
Make mashed potatoes, use a large can of drained corn, 16 oz.
shredded cheese.
Now layer your greased baking dish with the potatoes, corn,
Vegetable Protein mixture and vegan shredded cheese. (save some
cheese for the top)
Bake 30-45 minutes until hot.

So those are some of the ideas for using Vegetable Protein.
Basically anything you would use hamburger in, you can use
Vegetable Protein instead.
You can experiment and see what you like best.

CHAPTER SIX: RECIPES USING DOUGH

RECIPE: PIZZA OR CALZONE

Buy two balls of fresh pizza dough, most stores have this now, or buy it at a bakery.
The dough can be frozen. Just thaw them out, and they are ready to use.

For Pizza you need a cookie sheet or round pizza pan.
I suggest you use Crisco Vegetable Shortening, for some reason
The store brand shortening does not work as well.

Spread a thin layer of shortening on your pan. Preheat your over to 375 degrees.

For pizza you need two balls or two pounds of dough to make on large cookie sheet. Put the dough in the middle of the pan, grease your fingers a bit and spread the dough out covering the pan. (the shortening keeps the dough from rolling back)

If you ever used oil to do this, you will know exactly what I am talking about)
Once the dough is spread out, put pizza sauce on the dough. Spread it out evenly. Now add shredded cheese, usually 16 oz. will be enough. The stores have cheese substitutes that are really good. Now top off with your favorite items such as mushrooms, onions and peppers. You can sauté the toppings first, or put them on fresh. Bake until the bottom is brown and crispy and the cheese on top has melted.

Instead of dough you can use pita bread, just put on your sauce, cheese and toppings and bake until crispy. You can also make pizza without the cheese.

You can buy the low carb pita bread and use that if your watching your carbs.

Pizza with mushrooms, peppers and veggie pepperoni

CALZONE:

You can make one big calzone by putting two of the dough's together, or make two smaller ones.

Grease your cookie sheet, place you dough on the cookie sheet and spread it out, covering the bottom, like you did for the pizza.
Put on the sauce, cheese and fillings. Try some spinach, olives, broccoli, or mushrooms. I like to sauté everything first. But make sure It's cooled off before you put it on the dough or it will cause the dough to split open if it's still warm.

Then you are going to roll up the dough starting from the long side, fold it over to the middle about two inches and roll it up trying to fold in the ends as you go along. You will get better with it the more you make them.
Tuck the ends under and make sure the seam is on the bottom.
So you might have to flip it over so the seam is on the bottom.
Try not to overfill the calzone, as too much filling will cause it to leak out when cooking.

Bake it about 45 minutes. It should be nice and brown on the top.

Another option for making calzones is breaking off the dough into four or five sections, making single little calzones.
Roll out each little section, put on your sauce, cheese and filling and pull up the sides and connect it at the top. Flip them over so the seam is on the bottom.

FRIED GREEN PEPPERS

This is the way to make perfect fried green peppers.
My sister makes them the best. These are great to make up ahead of time for pizza and calzones. We love to use them in scrambled eggs.

Melt a stick of oleo in your frying pan or use olive oil. Prepare peppers by cutting into slices. Put the peppers in the pan and cover and cook on low to medium heat and stir until soft and done. You do not want to burn them, so watch the heat.
You do not need salt or pepper.

You can do the same with fresh mushrooms. But cook them in a separate pan.
Onions you can do the same, but do not cover them as if you do, you will get soggy onions. Below is a pizza with peppers, mushrooms and spinach.

SCALLION PANCAKES:

There are many way and techniques to make these pancakes and it's basically very easy. This is how I make them.

In a medium sized bowl put in 3 cups of flour
Add enough water to make a dough, but not too sticky.
Mix then knead the dough until soft.
Cover and let set aside for a half hour.
Then knead it again and roll out into a big circle.

Spread 2 teaspoons of sesame seed oil on top of the dough

Scallion Pancakes

Chop two bunches of green scallions and spread on top of dough
Use a rolling pin and press them in.

Then roll up the dough like a jellyroll, and cut into 2 inch slices.

Each section you can now roll out into a little circle about ¼ inch
thick. Fry each pancake in hot oil in a frying pan until browned on
both sides.
Cut each pancake when done into quarters and serve with soy sauce.

To make the soy sauce
In a bowl put ½ cup soy sauce
1 teaspoon of sugar and 1 teaspoon of sesame seed oil

Serve and enjoy!

RECIPE: LO-MEIN:

Buy Asian style noodles in the produce department.
First sauté the vegetables of your choice, such as onions, garlic, and peppers. You can add whatever you like.
When it's done, add one bag of fresh bean sprouts and stir until lightly cooked. Add a couple tablespoons of soy sauce while cooking.

While you are doing that, bring a pot of water to a boil. Then add your noodles. You need to separate them a little before you put them in the boiling water. Boil uncovered for about 3-4 minutes.
Drain and rinse with cool water.

Then add the noodles to the vegetables and add some more soy sauce, about one tablespoon, and 1 tablespoon of oyster sauce and stir until hot and the vegetables are mixed in with the noodles
You can put the noodles on a platter and top with fresh chopped scallions.

.

Personal Notes and Recipes:

Lo-Mein

STIR FRIED VEGETABLES WITH RICE:
Everyone should have a rice steamer, they are easy to use and you get perfect results.

I prefer Carolina brand jasmine rice. It has the best aroma and taste.

The standard measure to make rice in the steamer is one cup of rice to ¾ cups of water, and a dash of salt. Then just turn it on until it's done.
I usually use two cups of rice to 2 ½ cups of water and a teaspoon of salt. This makes enough for four people.

When its done, add some butter and fluff it up with a fork.

TO STIR FRY VEGETABLES:

Buy your favorite vegetables and cut them into small pieces.
Get your oil hot, then add the vegetables. Stir and cook until done to your desired tenderness. Add some soy sauce while cooking, adding a little oyster sauce will add more flavor to the vegetables.

You can also add some almonds or cashews to this dish. Either cook them with the vegetables or add when done. This will add some protein and essential oils to your dish.

Serve with hot rice.

Don't forget you can also make egg foo young, which is listed under the egg dishes.

Broccoli Rabe with Onion

BROCOLLI RABE WITH ONION:

Buy a bunch of Broccoli Rabe and cut in 2 inch lengths
Slice up 2 onions.
Heat some Sesame Seed Oil in a large frying pan and
Sauté 3 cloves of garlic minced then add the onions.
In the meantime soak about 10 Shitake Mushrooms, or use fresh,
Slice and add to vegetables and stir fry until tender
While cooking add 2 tablespoons soy sauce and 1 tab. Oyster Sauce.
Serve as a side dish or over rice

Summer Rice Paper Rolls

SUMMER RICE PAPER ROLLS:

Cut 8 oz. firm tofu in 8 slices and cut each slice in half. Dust with
Corn Starch and a little salt.

Set aside
Heat 1 tab. oil and cook tofu 2 -3 minutes per side adding Tamaria
Sauce or Soy Sauce to them. Brown and set aside to cool.

Prepare filling:
Grate 2 med. carrots
Slice two small zucchini in half lengthwise
1 cup assorted sprouts of your choice
use any fresh vegetables you would like.
A few fresh basil leaves (a few for each wrap)
set aside
then take your rice paper sheets and soften them in warm water and
remove carefully
place the rice paper on a plate and arrange the filling and then roll up
like a egg roll
spray a dish with non-stick spray and set rolls on the dish.

prepare sauce

mix well:
3 tab. peanut butter
2 tab. coconut milk or plain milk
2 tab. maple syrup
1 tab. rice vinegar
optional: crush fresh peanuts

if you want it spicy you can add some diced hot cherry peppers

I spread the sauce on the tofu, and put it in the wrap when I rolled
them.
Or you can use it as you eat it.
I also like this for a sauce that you can add to them as you eat them.
Mix in a little bowl: 1/4 cup vinegar,1/4 cup Tamari Sauce or soy
sauce, ½ tsp. sesame seed oil. Make it a little sweeter by adding
sugar or spice with a little chili paste. Arrange rolls and serve

Fresh Beansprouts

FRESH BEANSPROUTS:

Fresh Beansprouts: buy a package of beansprouts, heat ¼ cup of oil, and sauté a few minutes add some soy sauce and serve

CHAPTER EIGHT: 7 WAYS TO GET PROTEIN WITHOUT EATING MEAT

NUTS: All varieties of nuts: almonds, peanuts, cashews, pecans, hazelnuts. Peanut butter is an excellent source of protein with 4 grams per tablespoon. Watch the salt though: the USDA recommends choosing unsalted nuts to keep the sodium intake low.

SEEDS: Who knew they were good for you? Pumpkin, squash, sunflower, sesame and watermelon seeds. Many of these seeds provide upwards of 33 grams of protein per 100 gram serving.

BEANS: One of their remarkable qualities is a wealth of protein, especially black and garbanzo beans. Bean burgers are very good too.

SOY: tofu, soy milk, veggie burgers and tempeh. Tofu provides 20 grams of protein per half cup, whereas soy beans have 14 grams for the same amount.

SUPPLEMENTS AND BARS: A smoothie or energy bar is perfect for protein. Watch the sugar and fat, or your health "benefit" may turn into a net negative.

CEREAL: Cereals like Kashi Go Lean can also be good sources of protein.

SPINACH: Spinach provides protein as well as fiber and Vitamin A. Toss in some cheese and double up on the nutrition!

(Katie Fetting-Schlerf and article first printed in Full Circle's Good Food Life Blog)

Cinnamon Dipped Sugar Cookies

CINNAMON DIPPED SUGAR COOKIES:

Mix in a bowl:
½ cup butter
½ cup shortening
1 ½ cup sugar
beat in:
2 eggs, 2 tsp. cream of tartar, ¼ tsp. salt, 2 tsp. vanilla
then add:
2 ¾ cups flour
this should form a nice dough.
Shape into balls about the 2 inches round.
Roll each one is a mixture of sugar and cinnamon and bake 325
degrees for 20 minutes

Spicy Tomato Sauce on Angel Hair

SPICY TOMATO SAUCE:

In a large frying pan sauté 1 cup chopped onion and 2 cloves of garlic
Add 3 large fresh tomatoes chopped
1 tsp. basil
1 tsp. oregano
cook until the tomatoes are softened
add 1 package of Taco seasoning
salt and pepper
1 jar of your favorite spaghetti sauce
cook until hot

Cook one pound of Angel Hair Pasta
Drain and melt a few pats of butter on top.
Put your pasta on a large serving dish and top with
Sauce

Hot Pepper Sauce

HOT PEPPER SAUCE:

Dice 1 large red pepper and 1 large yellow pepper and one large onion and sauté in olive oil.
Prepare 2 cups textured vegetable protein in a bowl, adding 2 cups of stock and 1 tablespoon of gravy master
Sauté in hot olive oil adding salt and pepper and one cube of Sasson Seasoning
Add the peppers and onions
Then chop up two tomatoes and add and stir together until hot

In a large kettle put in two jars of your favorite spaghetti sauce, the above mixture and add 2 teaspoons red pepper flakes stir simmer on low heat for about ten minutes

Cook Angel Hair or your favorite pasta and serve

Hot Pepper Sauce Simmering

CHAPTER TEN: GREG HODDE

GREG'S COOKIES:

Buy a package of your favorite refrigerated cookie dough and follow the directions! Easy as that!

Halloween Cookies

Reindeer Cookies

Tree Cookies

Ghost cookies

Tomato Soup and Grilled Cheese

TOMATO SOUP AND GRILLED CHEESE:

Take two pieces of bread, butter one side on each piece
Place 1 slice of vegan cheese in between the unbuttered bread sides.
(use earth balance butter or any non-dairy spread)
heat your frying pan, and grill the sandwich ,butter side down, until
browned on both sides
serve with tomato soup

Elderberry tea

ELDERBERRY TEA:

This tea is great for cold and flu season.
In addition to flavor, it has medicinal properties. Elderberry tea has been used for centuries to clear sinuses and alleviate the symptoms of the common cold and flu. To use elderberry tea medicinally, simmer the tea and drink it three times daily.

Place 3 teaspoons of dried elderberry flowers or berries into a strainer. Bring 1 cup of water to a simmer. Place the tea strainer into the water and let set for about 15 minutes. Remove the strainer.
Pour the tea into a cup and allow it to cool for a few minutes before drinking. Add honey, lemon or sugar if desired.

Fettuccine Alfredo

FETTUCCINE ALFREDO:

Cook 1 pound of fettuccine as directed on package.

Set aside

Buy one jar of Alfredo sauce and follow directions to heat.

Pour over fettuccine and serve

A nice side is garlic bread and a tossed salad

CHAPTER ELEVEN: JACQUELINE SEWELL

"A few choice recipes from "The Notorious Cook"

Stuffed Mushrooms ready to bake

STUFFED MUSHROOMS: – "out of this world"

Purchase 12 large stuffing mushrooms. (these are the large white ones, but if not available smaller ones will be fine. or try using any type of mushroom you like.

Remove the stems. Set aside the mushroom caps. Then to make the stuffing:

Mince 3 cloves of garlic

Crumble a 12 oz. package of blue cheese

And make about 7 cups of bread crumbs.

(a food processor blender will make bread crumbs) do not use the canned bread crumbsMelt 2 sticks of butter, add to garlic, blue cheese and bread crumbs.

Add a little mile to make a moist stuffing

Mix well and pack the caps nice and full.

Bake at 350 degrees 45 minutes.

(instead of discarding the stems, they can be sautéed and used in other dishes.)

SPINACH STUFFED MUSHROOMS;

This is another quick and easy way to make tasty mushrooms.

Mix one box of a herbed stuffing mix, follow directions on box, set aside stuffing. Buy about 12 stuffing mushrooms and remove stems and chop up fine. sauté with 3 cloves of diced garlic with a little oil.

Add to stuffing. Cook one package frozen chopped spinach, drain well and cool. Add to stuffing. Then mix in 1 cup of shredded cheese and 1 cup of grated parmesan cheese. Once mixed, pack each mushroom with the stuffing. Bake 350 degrees for about 20 minutes.

Italian Soup with grated cheese

SIMPLY WONDERFUL ITALIAN SOUP:

This soup is excellent when served very hot with garlic bread and sprinkled with parmesan cheese.

Put 3 large cans of whole tomatoes in a bowl. (Crush the tomatoes by hand).

Then chop one large green pepper and one large red pepper

Mince 5 cloves of garlic

6 medium summer squash diced, 6 medium zucchini squash diced,3 stalks celery diced

Place all vegetables and tomatoes in a large kettle.

Then add:

2 tablespoons fennel seeds

¼ cup of sugar, ½ teaspoon salt, 1 teaspoon Italian seasoning

¼ teaspoon black pepper and cook slowly until vegetables are tender.

You can also make this in a crockpot.

You may also add 1 cup of elbow macaroni in the beginning of cooking.

Baked Stuffed Tomatoes

BAKED STUFFED TOMATOES:

These crabmeat and cheddar tomatoes are scrumptiously delicious.

This recipe may be doubled if needed.

16 medium tomatoes-slice off the top/not the bottom/scoop out the

center's and save. Save centers and juice/put in a food processer or blender and Blend. Save to add to filling

To Make The Filling:

Use 8-10 cups of breadcrumbs. Make your own crumbs, using white

Bread, then add to the crumbs:

2 cups of grated sharp cheddar cheese

the saved tomato centers

1 pound of imitation shredded crabmeat

add 2 sticks melted oleo to make a moist stuffing and mix.

pack and fill the tomatoes, then place them in a greased

cupcake tin and bake until browed and well done.

350 degrees about 45 minutes

(you can also use this stuffing mix for stuffed mushrooms)

Caso Dip

EASY CASO DIP FOR SCOOPING:

You will need 1 pound of Velveta brand cheese
A small can of Rotel Tomatoes either mild or hot.
(these are in the shopping area where you buy canned tomatoes)

Heat tomatoes to a simmer and add the Velveta brand cheese that
you have cut up into small chunks.
Simmer slowly stirring until the cheese melts.
Serve warm with scoop chips or even mix with elbow macaroni for a
different side dish.

Zucchini Squash Boats

ZUCCHINI SQUASH BOATS:

Buy one or two large zucchini and cut in half and scoop out the centers.
One box of Stove Top Herb Flavored Stuffing mix. Put in a large bowl.
Mix in 2 cups white bread crumbs and add it to the stuffing mix.

Chop and dice one onion and add to mix.
Melt one stick of oleo and add to mix
And 1 tablespoon of poultry seasoning.
Mix together.

Then cook:
2 stalks diced celery, 1 carrots diced, 3-4 cups of water
cook until vegetables are tender.

Add 1 tablespoons soup granules or cubes. You can use vegetable flavor or chicken if you choose. (health food stores do carry chicken and beef flavored cubes that are non-meat)

Cool and add to crumbs to make a nice moist stuffing.
Stuff each zucchini with the stuffing mixture.
Place in a greased baking dish and cover with foil.
Bake 350 degrees for about 45 minutes.
Some people like ketchup served with it.

Pumpkin Spice Bars

PUMPKIN SPICE BARS:

MIX:
4 eggs
1 cup of oil
1 can of pumpkin
2 cups of flour
2 tsps. baking powder
1 tsp. baking soda
½ tsp. cloves
1 tsp. nutmeg

½ tsp. ginger
¾ tsp. salt, Mix well then add ¾ raisins

Pour batter onto a large greased cookie sheet.
Bake 350 for about 25 minutes.
Cool and frost

BUTTER CREAM FROSTING:

Pour one box of confectioners sugar in a bowl.
Add one stick of soft oleo and one tsp.vanilla extract.
Add a little soy milk or coconut milk and start beating it with an
electric mixer, adding a little more soy milk or coconut milk until its
thick enough for frosting.
(if you add too much milk, you can add more frosting sugar until its
thick enough)

Personal Notes and Recipes:

Apple Cake Squares

JACKIE'S APPLE OR BLUEBERRY CAKE SQUARES:

Use a large cookie sheet for this.

Mix in a large bowl:
¼ cup water
2 cups sugar
4 eggs
2 tsp. vanilla extract
½ tsp. salt
4 sticks of melted oleo

Then add:
4 cups of flour
1 tsp. cinnamon
1 tsp. nutmeg
mix well
Use half of the batter to cover the bottom of your greased cookie sheet
Open 2 cans of apples or blueberries and arrange on top of batter,
Cover with remaining batter and bake 350 until browned
(if you use blueberries omit the nutmeg)

Blueberry Bread

JACKIE'S BLUEBERRY BREAD:

Mix in a large bowl:

2 ½ cups sugar
2 tsp. salt
1 1/2 tsp. baking soda
1 yellow cake mix (follow directions on box and add it to bowl)
then mix in:
2 ½ tab. Oil
2 tsp. vanilla extract
4 eggs
1 cup of milk or coconut milk or soy
Mix well.

Then mix in 4 cups of flour or more until you have a thick batter. You
might need to add more milk if it's too thick.

Then stir in 2 pints of fresh blueberries or 4 cups of frozen.
Pour batter into greased bread pans 3.4 full and bake 350 degrees
until done about 45-60 minutes
Makes about 6 loaves or 24 muffins.
Frost if you like. (shown below)

Jackie's Devil Chocolate Cake

JACKIE'S DEVIL CHOCOLATE CAKE:

Beat in a bowl with a mixer:

½ cup shortening
½ cup baking cocoa
1 ½ cups sugar
2 eggs
½ tsp. salt
1 cup hot
1 tsp. vanilla extract

Then add:

1 ½ cups flour
1 tsp. baking soda
1 tsp. baking powder

mix well and put in a greased cake pan.
Bake 350 degrees about 35 minutes

Frost with butter cream frosting when it's cool

Zucchini Bread

JACKIE'S ZUCCHINI BREAD:

(makes 8-9 loaves)

In a large bowl mix:

10 eggs
1 cup of oil
2 tsp. vanilla
2 cups of grated zucchini
and add enough milk to moisten

Then add:
1 yellow cake mix/add the dry contents
Plus:
4 cups of sugar
2 tsp. cinnamon
2 tsp. baking soda
4 tsp. baking powder
2 tsp. salt
1 tsp. nutmeg
½ tsp. cloves
mix and then add:
4-6 cups of flour as you mix add enough flour to make a nice batter.

Hint: you can put the eggs and cut up squash in a blender to grind.
Also as a option, you can add two carrots and two bananas to the mix

Grease bread pans and fill each one ¾ full of batter.
Bake 350 degrees for about 45-60 minutes until done.

Oatmeal Raisin Cookies

JACKIE'S OATMEAL RAISIN COOKIES:

In a large bowl mix together:

1 cup of butter
1 cup of sugar
1 cup of brown sugar
2 eggs
1 tsp. vanilla extract
1 tsp. salt.

Then mix in (use a large bowl)

3 cups of oats
1 cup of raisins
2 cups of flour
Mix and drop by the tablespoon onto a greased cookie sheet
Bake 350 degrees 8-10 minutes
You can also add coconut flakes or chocolate chips instead of raisins

Lemon Bars

LEMON BARS:

Mix in a large bowl:

4 eggs
2 cups of sugar
½ tsp. salt
6 tab. Lemon juice
½ cup butter
1 tsp. baking powder
set this mixture to the side.
In a separate bowl:
Mix:
2 cups of flour
½ cup soft butter
½ cup confectioners sugar

now press this mixture onto the bottom of a greased cookie sheet.
Bake 325 degrees for 20 minutes and let it cool.
Then when its cool, pour the other mixture over it and spread evenly
across the top.
Bake 20 minutes and cool.
Sprinkle confectioners sugar on top when cool.

Apple Pie Squares

JACKIE'S FAMOUS APPLE PIE SQUARES:

In a large bowl:
Mix 4 cups of flour
2 cups of shortening
2 tsp. salt.
Mix with a fork until flour and shortening are combined
Then add a little ice cold want until a dough forms.
Make sure it sticks together and you can form it into a ball but you don't want it sticky.
On a rolling board, or you can use your clean counter top. Put a cup of flour on the surface, and you will be making this using a large cookie sheet.
Put the ball of dough onto the counter top and use a rolling pin and roll out, you want it to be the size of your cookie sheet plus about two inches bigger so the dough will go over the edges. When its this size, fold the dough in half and place on the cookie sheet and open it up.
If you get any cracks just push it together again.
Put this to the side.

Now you want to peal about 12 large apples and slice them onto the dough you have on the cookie sheet.
Once that is done mix 2 cups of sugar with 2 tab. of cinnamon and 1 tsp. of nutmeg. Spread this mixture over the apples.

Now repeat the steps making the dough for the top.
When its rolled out, place on top of the apples.
Fold the edges under all the way around.

Now mix together: 1 egg and ½ cup of water.
Use a pastry brush and brush the top of the dough.
Mix ½ cup of sugar and 1 tsp. of cinnamon and sprinkle on top.
Bake 350 degrees for one hour.

Another thing you can do once you make your pie dough
Is this fancy apple treat.

Roll out your dough, into a circle about 8 inches across.
Core and peel one apple and place in the center of the dough
Fill the core will sugar and cinnamon.
Now pull up the dough around the apple and pinch at the top.
Use the egg and water mixture and apply with the pastry brush.
Sprinkle on cinnamon and sugar.
Bake 350 degrees for about 40 minutes.

Or use the same dough recipe and make an apple pie
Follow the same basic direction except you will be using pie plates.
The picture below is apple pie with no sugar or cinnamon on the top

CHAPTER TWELVE: YOUR FOOD JOURNAL

Food journals are a great way to keep track of what you eat.
It helps you actually see what you are eating.
Diet centers use this method to help us see where we might be falling short, and also to see how well we do when we eat healthy.

I found a fun way to keep a food journal that is creative and maybe it can bring out the "child" in us all that we sometimes miss so much!

What you will need for this journal is your journal or a notebook and a box of colored pencils.

Each day in your journal, enter the date and if your on a diet you can record your weight.

Whatever you eat for the day, you will draw a cute picture of it in your journal. Use you colored pencils and get creative!

So far today I have a blue cup drawn that I had my coffee in and two eggs.

The goal for this type of journal is trying to eat less meat.

Have fun, draw cool pictures, and you just might find yourself an aspiring artist.

Here is a picture of one of my journal pages:

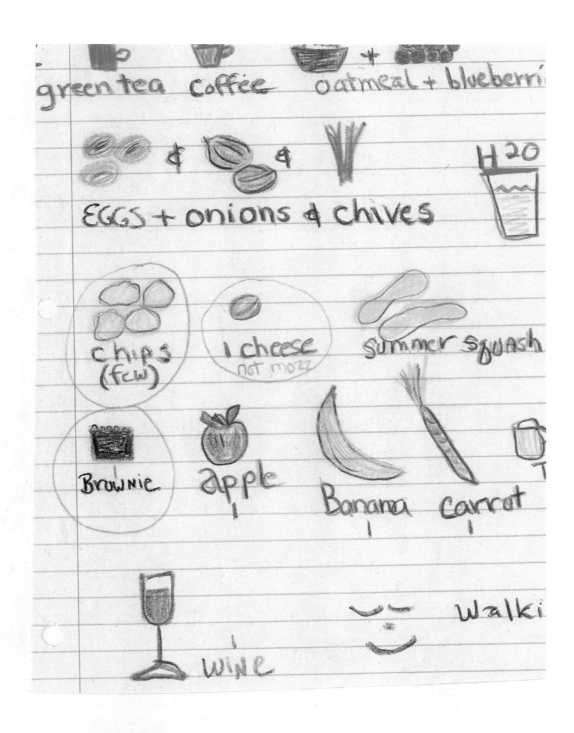

green tea   coffee   oatmeal + blueberri

EGGS + onions & chives   H20

chips
(fcw)

1 cheese
not mozz

summer squash

Brownie   apple   Banana   carrot

wine   Walki

"Did you ever consider that many recipes ever written by men and women,
throughout history, might as well have been written in actual blood? Blood shed

by the millions of innocent victims, the animals. Besides making blood pudding, they could have used some of it for ink. Today the food companies try not to waste any parts of the animals,(profit margins) so they can make more money.

For example, they use the blood from the cows and feed it to the calves as a milk

substitute. I learned that from the Dvd "Frankencow," it's is a documentary on the food processing of meats in Canada and United States.

Some other good dvd's to watch are:

Food, Inc.

The Witness

Peaceable Kingdom

Forks over Knives

Fed Up

Youtube videos:

Peta presents "Glass Walls" narrated by Paul McCartney

Food That Kills presented by Dr. Michael Klaper

CHAPTER THIRTEEN: VICKIE-JULIAN AND BOB HUGHES

BOB'S PORTOBELLO BURGER:

In a frying pan add minced garlic, onion, and a small handful of baby spinach with 1 tbs. of olive oil, sauté over medium heat.
Put 4 Portobello mushrooms on top, topside up. Season to taste.
I used salt, pepper, garlic powder, and basil, Worcestershire Sauce.
Put more spinach on top. Cover tightly and let it cook down. The spinach will almost disappear. After 15–20 min, you can flip the mushrooms and let it cook covered again for 10 min or so. Remove lid and flip mushroom back over.
cook until liquid in the pan is almost gone. Press mushrooms with a spatula to remove excess juices. Place a piece of Swiss cheese on top. Remove from pan when the cheese has melted.

VICKIE'S BUG EYES:

Ritz Crackers, peanut butter and red seedless grapes. Spread peanut butter, (I recommend Teddy brand) over the cracker. Take a red grape and cut it in half lengthwise. Place both halves flat side down, side by side on top of the cracker. They are delicious!

CHOPPED WALNUTS AND RAISINS:

A snack I enjoy anytime of day or evening is a mixture of chopped walnuts and raisins. You get the crunch with a touch of sweetness, that are unprocessed! Plus, you get a good dose of protein, iron, potassium and carbs for energy.Plus these will travel well in a small plastic container and they are easy to eat on the go. A great pick me up snack when your dreaming about dinner mid afternoon.

CHEESE AND ALMONDS:

Another snack that's good for picking on are slices of Cabot's 50%* less fat sharp cheese. I cut the slices very thin and place them around the edge of a small sandwich plate lengthwise pointing to the center of the plate. Then I place a handful of Emerald's Cocoa Roast Almonds** in the middle. It looks decorative and tasty! Kind of looks like a sunflower!

Along with these snacks, I like to enjoy a nice, hot cup of decaf tea in the evenings! To help wind down I go for a chamomile tea, green tea or if I feel a cold coming on, a cup of Echinacea tea to the rescue!

Along with the wonderful flavors, the scent of these teas will also relax you and get you ready for a peaceful sleep.

Herb tea, peanut butter on apple slices and walnuts

CHAPTER FOURTEEN: BARBARA JEAN NAGLE

Tomato Stew

TOMATO STEW:

Progresso Soups makes a tasty tomato starter. It's great for many recipes.
I found it tasty for this tomato stew.
Pour 3 cans of Progresso Tomato Soup Started into a large kettle.
Cook a bag of frozen stew vegetables, there are many different brands. They
usually contain carrots, onions, celery and potato. Follow cooking directions for
the vegetables and drain well. Add to the tomato soup.
You can add other vegetables if you like.
Then just heat and serve.
Try adding some non-dairy grated cheese and crackers on the side.
If you have never tried the non-dairy grated cheese, it actually has a better taste
then the dairy grated cheese.
I serve this soup with grilled cheese on the side using Sesame Seed Ezekiel 4:9
bread.

Favorite no steak dinner:mushrooms, broccoli, potato, butternut squash

FAVORITE NO-STEAK DINNER

This is one of my favorites, and it is so tasty and satisfying.

I love instant mashed potatoes, but you can use homemade if you prefer.

I make mashed potatoes and sauté the Portobello mushrooms.

I also might fry green and red peppers, using Virgin Coconut Oil.
Then add a green vegetable, like broccoli on the side.

You can make any combination you like but eating the mashed potatoes with the vegetables tastes so good you won't even miss the steak.

When you sauté the Portobello mushroom with garlic and salt and pepper and do not over cook them, they have the same flavor as a steak when done.
So if you buy them either slice them thick or buy them pre-sliced.

Spicy Tofu Chili

SPICY TOFU CHILI

fry and saute one pound of firm tofu
to do this: slice the tofu and lightly coat with cornstarch.
fry in oil, until crisp.
cool and slice into little squares

Put tofu in a large kettle
add 2 cups of vegetable stock
1 packages of your favorite chili spice
1 cup cooked or canned lima beans
1 can of white beans
1 teaspoon of tumeric
1 bunch of chives chopped

heat to a boil and shut off
serve as a soup or serve over rice

Pumpkin Soup:

In a pan sauté 1 medium chopped onion in 2 tabs. Olive oil.
Add 2 cans stock.
Set aside.
You can either use a can of prepared pumpkin or use a real pumpkin.
If you use a real pumpkin, cut into quarters and remove seeds.
Boil pumpkin until soft. Scoop cooked pumpkin from shell and add to the stock.
Once its cooled, put the stock in blender and blend until smooth
Place blended stock into a pan and add:
1 tsp. salt
¼ tsp. cinnamon
1/8 tsp. ginger
1/8 tsp. pepper
and heat.
Once it's hot but not boiling add 1 cup milk substitute.
Heat but do not boil.

Noodles with Kale

NOODLES WITH KALE:

Buy a package of lo-mein noodles.

First add 2 tablespoons olive oil to your large frying pan
Sauté 2 large onions with salt and pepper
Once they are browned, add 2 cups frozen chopped kale or you can use fresh.
Sauté until tender.
Then bring to a boil 5 cups of water and add your lo-mein noodles
Cook for about 3 minutes, drain and add to the onions and kale
Stir and mix, add 2 tablespoons soy sauce mix and serve

Bok Choy

BOK CHOY:

Buy about 2-3 pounds of Bok Choy, either the small heads or a large head.
If you buy the large head of bok choy you will need to chop it up into smaller sections
Add ¼ cup of oilive oil in a large kettle and add the Bok Choy, cook and stir until done. Add salt and better to taste.

Healthy Cookies

HEALTHY COOKIES:

In a large bowl combine:
3 sticks butter or oleo, 4 eggs, 1 cup brown sugar,
1 cup white sugar, 1 tsp. salt, 3 tsp. vanilla, 2 tsp. nutmeg
2 tsp. lemon extract, or almond extract, 1 tsp. baking soda
beat with a mixer.

Add and stir in:

1 can pumpkin
1 cup raisins
1/2 cup sesame seeds
1 bag cranberries
1/2 cup flaxseed milled
1 cup walnut halves
2 carrots (put in a food processor, or put in blender with 1/4
cup water to chop, or chop them fine)
1 package chocolate chips, or cocoa chips
3 cups oatmeal (not quick)
1 package coconut flakes (the package is usually about 12
oz.)
mix and then add 2 cups flour.

drop by ice cream scooper onto greased cookie sheet,
flatten down a bit, use a little water on your fingers to do so.
bake 325 until browned on bottom.

this recipe is adjustable, you can add other things or take
away. Try adding chopped apples, or other kinds of nuts.
but the sesame seeds and flax seeds give your recipe
healthy proteins and many other good things.

Coconut Oil

Did you know Coconut Oil is awesome?

The health benefits of coconut oil include hair care, skin care, stress relief, maintaining cholesterol levels, weight loss, increased immunity, proper digestion and metabolism, relief from kidney problems, heart diseases, high blood pressure, diabetes, HIV and cancer, dental care, and bone strength. These benefits of oil can be attributed to the presence of Lauric Acid, Capric Acid and Caprylic Acid and its properties such as antimicrobial, antioxidant, anti-fungal, antibacterial and soothing properties.

Cabbage, Potato and Carrots

MEATLESS CORNED BEEF AND CABBAGE:

Do you love corned beef and cabbage but really love the cabbage and potatoes and carrots more than the meat? To me the vegetables topped with a butter substitute, salt and pepper, are the best part of the meal.
So make it without the meat!

But a nice green cabbage, quarter it and place in a large kettle of water.
Add carrots and potatoes (red potatoes are great and you don't have to peel them) you can also add yams.
Bring to a boil and then just simmer until all the vegetables are done.

Healthy Fruit Drink

HEALTHY FRUIT DRINK:

Peel a grapefruit and put it in a blender (do not add water) blend well and then add:
1 peeled orange, 1 apple and one banana and 1 cup of cranberry juice and blend well. (do not remove seeds, its all healthy for you)
you can also add a tablespoon of honey.
If you have allergies its good to buy a local honey and use it daily as a sweetner, it will help you adapt to the pollens in your area and make your allergies less bothersome.

This beverage contains pectin which as the ability to lower both bad cholesterol and triglyceride levels.
It also contains lycopene, which is a great fighter against toxins.

Some people cannot eat grapefruit while taking certain medications so check if your not sure.

Grapefruit also contains vitamin C, A, D, E, calcium, magnesium, zinc, copper, iron and phosphorus.

You can add other fruits of your choice. Blueberries are good too and add more antitoxins.

Drinking a homemade juice is so much better for you then the juice you buy in the store with so much added sugar.

Taco Bowls

TACO BOWLS;

This has become one of my favorites!
You can now buy a taco kit with little taco bowls.
I use the spices in the kit except I use textured vegetable protein instead of the hamburger.
So for one recipe, mix two cups of textured vegetable protein and add enough warm water to moisten and add two tablespoons of gravy master and mix.

Chop one onion and 3 cloves of garlic.
Saute' until lightly browned and add salt and pepper.
Now add the vegetable protein and follow the directions on your taco kit box.

On the side serve chopped lettuce and cubed tomatoes. Use with the toppings of your choice.
I like the vegan grated cheese or a vegan mozzarella shredded cheese, and hot sauce.
The little taco bowls can be heated in the over to make them more crunchy.
Now for your next day's lunch, reheat in the oven.

This is something new I just discovered. It's excellent and you can use it in your spaghetti sauce. Eat these sausage plain or serve on the side.

Stuffed Shells and Sauce

STUFFED SHELLS AND SAUCE:

You will need:
1 box of shells
your favorite spaghetti sauce
1 pound of ricotta cheese
12 oz. shredded mozzarella cheese (a good substitute for mozzarella or cheddar shreads is "Daiya Brand" shredded cheese)

In a large bowl mix the ricotta and mozzarella, mix in 4 eggs, 2 cloves of minced garlic, 2 tsp. parsley, 1 tsp. salt, 1 tsp. pepper and mix well.

Cook the shell in boiling water as directed on the box.
Cool the shells when done.

When cook, fill each shell with the cheese mixture. Lay them in a baking dish that has been sprayed with baking spray or rub olive oil on the bottom of the dish. Put some sauce on the bottom. Lay the filled shells carefully in the pan. Cover with sauce, cover them with foil an bake about 45 minutes 350 degrees.

A salad on the side would be nice. The one I have pictured is made with:

Iceberg lettuce
Cherry tomatoes
Celery
Sliced zucchini squash
Sliced summer squash
Onions
Sliced baby carrots

Fresh Salad

Portobello Stuffed Mushrooms

PORTOBELLO STUFFED MUSHROOM:

Take the large top portions of Portobello mushrooms.
Place in a baking dish.
Cover the top with shredded cheese, and a slice tomato and place on top of each mushroom. Sprinkle with salt and pepper and put a few teaspoons of balsamic vinaigrette over the top of each one.
Cover with foil and bake for ½ hour at 325 degrees.

Vegetable Tofu Soup

VEGETABLE TOFU SOUP:

5 cans of vegetable soup stock

Put in a large kettle and start to heat.
And add:

1 can mixed vegetables (carrots, peas and corn)
1 package fresh collard greens
1 chopped onion
bring to a nice simmer and then lower the heat. Cook for about 30 minutes until collards are tender.

During the cooking time add:
1 tsp. ground red curry
1 tsp. ground green curry
1 tsp. ground yellow curry
1 tsp. garlic powder
1 tsp. black pepper

At the end, add one package of Tofu, cut into cubes.
For a more meaty texture slice your Tofu into thin slices or small cubes and freeze. Then add to your soup once it's frozen. Freezing it changes the texture to make it chewy and meat like.

Another good item to add is meatballs (found in the vegetarian section of your supermarket.

You can add different vegetables if you prefer. Some options are:
Cabbage, potato, green beans, kidney beans or dry beans. A few cut up fresh tomatoes would add a nice touch.

Serve in a bowl with chopped chives.

Pasta Veggie Salad

PASTA VEGGIE SALAD:

One 16 ounce package of Radiator Pasta or any pasta of your choice
Cook as directed, rinse and cool with cold water and set aside.

Prepare:
¼ cup fresh asparagus diced
¼ cup fresh green beans sliced
½ cup cherry tomatoes cut in half
1 small onion chopped fine
½ bunch fresh green chives chopped.

Mix with cooled pasta.
Then add:
¾ cup Miracle Whip or a non-dairy mayo.
You can now by a mayonnaise made from grapes which is actually very good for
you and lowers your cholesterol.
1 cup Balsamic Vinaigrette

mix well, cover and refrigerate

You might need to add more mayo and vinaigrette if it's too dry.

Zucchini Lasagna

ZUCCHINI LASAGNA:

Cook until tender: about 3 pounds of sliced zucchini that has been cut
Lengthwise into about ¼ inch thick slice (do not over cook)
Drain and save.

Fry 1 cup of chopped onions and add 1 cup of textured vegetable protein and 2 cups of vegetable stock and 1 tablespoon of gravy master. Cook and mix for a few minutes.
Then add to the veg. protein mixture:

3 large can diced tomatoes
1 can tomato paste
1 jar of your favorite spaghetti sauce
2 cloves of garlic chopped
½ tsp. oregano
½ tsp. basil
½ tsp. thyme
½ cup of water
½ tsp. pepper
Bring to a boil, reduce heat and simmer for about ten minutes.
Set this aside.

In a bowl mix:

16 ounces cottage cheese or ricotta
2 eggs, 1 cup mozzarella shredded cheese, 1 tsp. flour
(when recipes are calling for cheese, you can buy non-dairy cheese in the vegan section of your supermarket)

In a large baking dish, spoon some of the sauce on the bottom.
Then layer half of the zucchini and all of the cheese mixture.
Top with the rest of the sauce and zucchini layers
Put the rest of the sauce on top of this.

Bake uncovered at 350 degrees for 30 minutes. Sprinkle ½ cup shredded cheese on top and bake a few minutes more until it melts.

Let stand 10 minutes before serving.

Crockpot Balsamic Tofu Soup

CROCKPOT BALSAMIC TOFU SOUP:

Buy a package of firm Tofu
Slice thin and spread out on a tray and freeze. This will give you a meaty texture.
Once its frozen, remove from freezer (about 1 hour)

In a bowl mix:

1 tsp. garlic powder
1 tsp. basil
1 tsp. salt
½ tsp. pepper
2 tsps. minced onion
add Tofu to this mixture and shake to cover spices onto Tofu.
Set aside.

In the crockpot, put 2 tablespoons olive oil, 4 cloves of chopped garlic and place tofu mixture on top.

Pour in ½ cup Balsamic Vinegar
1 can vegetable stock
Cover and cook on med high for 30 minutes
Sprinkle fresh parsley on top when done
Serve over steamed rice.
You can also add other vegetables to this dish.
A can of tomato soup can also be added.

Eggplant Parmesan

FAVORITE EGGPLANT PARMESAN:

Quick and easy (pictured served with home fried potatoes and
Fresh asparagus)
Buy one large Eggplant
Cut off ends and slice thick slice about ½ inch each.
Take a large cookie sheet and spray a good coat of oil on it or rub with olive oil.
Lay down the slice of eggplant
Bake at 350 for about 20 minutes, when bottom is browned remove from over
and flip them over.
On the top of each slice of eggplant, spoon on your favorite tomato sauce. I find a
chunky tomatoes sauce is the best. Then put about 2 tsp. vegan grated
parmesan cheese on top of the sauce
Return the eggplants to the oven and bake an additional 20 minutes.

Homemade Ravioli

HOMEMADE RAVIOLI:

To make your dough:

Put two cups of flour in a bowl.
Make a well in the center of the flour and add
3 egg yolks, 2 teaspoons of salt and mix well.
Then mix in water, by adding about a 1 tablespoon at a time and mix until the
dough is stiff but easy to roll out.

Divide the dough into four equal parts. Roll out one section at a time to about ¼ inch thick on a floured surface.

In a separate bowl mix your filling:
You can make up your own filling but this is a good one.

Cook 1 package of frozen chopped spinach as directed, then drain and cool.
Mix into this 16 ounces ricotta cheese.
2 tsps. chopped garlic
salt and pepper
2 eggs and mix well.
Or you can make up any type of filling, a spicy veggie mix is also tasty for these.

Use a round cookie or biscuit cutter to cut out the circle of dough.
So cut out your circles.
Then in the center of each circle place a tablespoon of filling. Place another circle on top and use a fork to connect the edges together. If you flour the fork between pressing down the edges the dough will not stick.

Once you have made all of your ravioli's, you will need to bring a kettle of water to a boil. You can boil 6 at a time for about five minutes. Remove and drain and serve with your favorite sauce.

You can also make the ravioli and freeze on a cookie sheet.
Once frozen you can remove them and store in a freezer bag and cook as needed.

Turmeric Cake

RECIPE: TURMERIC CAKE

    3 cups flour, 2/3 cup sugar
    1 tbsp. turmeric, ¼ tsp. of salt
    1 ¾ cups unsweetened shredded coconut
    ¾ cup fresh cranberries, ¼ tsp. of salt
    ¾ cup coconut oil
    1 ¾ cups sweetened almond, coconut or soy milk
    1 tbsp. tahini (sesame paste)

Preheat over 325 degrees. Grease your baking dish
Mix all flour, sugar, turmeric and coconut, cranberries and salt.
Then add oil and milk and stir together, do not over mix
Spoon batter into the baking dish.
Bake about 45 minutes, until knife comes out of center clean
Once cooled, lightly frost and top with shredded almonds.
You can also do a substitution for the coconut.

Jalapeno Peppers with Cream Cheese

JALAPENO PEPPERS WITH CREAM CHEESE:

These are easy to make and are great for a snack.
Buy about 12 large jalapeno peppers.
Cut off the tops and slice in half, use a spoon to remove all the seeds.
Fill each one with vegan cream cheese. Place in a greased baking dish and cover with foil. Bake at 325 degrees for about 20 minutes until the peppers are soft.
Cool and serve. I like them cold with hot coffee in the morning.

Quick and Easy Dinner

QUICK AND EASY DINNER:
A easy and quick dinner:

For one bowl, slice fresh cucumbers and tomatoes

Fry tofu with oil and garlic then top with soy sauce and fry till browned. (bowl # 2)

Boil a sweet potato, when it's done slice in half and top with melted butter, salt and pepper (bowl # 3) (Can't Believe It's Not Butter)

Sauté a package of bok choy in melted butter, garlic and soy sauce, slice in fresh mushrooms and sauté until tender. Add salt and pepper. (bowl # 4)

An amazing quick and healthy meal.

Lemon Loaf

LEMON LOAF:

In a large bowl mix together:
3 eggs
1 ¼ cup sugar
½ cup of oleo or butter (vegan, or a substitute)
2 tsp. vanilla
put one whole lemon in a blender and blend well. (do not peel)
Then add to the bowl:
½ cup oil

1 tsp. lemon extract
½ cup water
blend well.
Then add 2 cups of flour
½ tsp. baking soda
½ tsp. baking powder
½ tsp. salt
blend.
Pour batter into two greased bread pans. Bake 325 degrees until done.
Cool and frost with a lemon frosting.

Celery Stuffed with Cream Cheese and Olives

STUFFED CELERY;

1 Package 16 oz. of cream cheese,(vegan) softened
place in a bowl and mash
add 3 Tab. juice from a jar of green olives
then dice about 15 olives and mix with the cream cheese.
Take some stalks of celery and cut into about 3 inch sections and fill
each section with the cream cheese mixture.
Chill and serve

Crockpot Meatballs

CROCKPOT MEATBALLS:

I like to use the meatless meatballs pictured in the photo, but you can use any brand you like.

In a large kettle, sauté 1 chopped onion, 3 Tab. olive oil and 3 cloves of garlic diced. Once these are lightly browned I add two packages of the meatballs and cook and stir for about 5 minutes.

Then mix with two jars of your homemade sauce or jar sauce.

Place in your crockpot and heat.

I like to serve these with Italian bread or rolls

I have bought the veggie style meatballs, and have found some that actually taste better than the "meat" meatballs you can buy in the grocery store.

Fry a onion and some garlic in olive oil, and then sauté the veggie meatballs in that for added flavor. Another product that is very good is Falafel. It comes in many varieties such as patties and meatballs.

Then I add them to my sauce. Believe me they are really good.

But If I tell my kids, those are veggie meatballs, they will not like them, and say what's in that?

I tell them it's made from soy, soy protein, spices and vegetables. That of course is disgusting to them, and they spit them out, but on the other hand, if they were made from meat and you answered that question, "oh they are made from cows, and spices." Then, that is fine. Now isn't that weird? But if I actually brought home a live cow, and killed it and cooked it, they would hate me forever!

So how can eating a dead cow, be better then eating something made with vegetables? Like what is worse? Eating something dead or a plant? Killing a living animal and eating it, or eating a plant?

I think it all goes back to how we are brought up and what we are use to.

So, here is a question, I am walking along the road and I am starving, and there is a dead squirrel on the road, just hit, and someone also left a bag of apples out by the side of the road. Now, do I run and grab the dead squirrel and cook him up, or eat the apples?

When I was a kid, my dad would have eaten both! But now, what if there was a bag of apples on the side of the road and a live squirrel sitting there and eating the apples? Do you eat the apples and share them with the squirrel, and let him live or kill the squirrel and eat him too? So many choices!

So how you live your life and the choices you make are your own. But I hope you choose to share the apples with the squirrel. And if the squirrel was already dead, show some respect and bury it. Some people reason that, if the animal is already dead, so why not buy it to eat, well, even though you are not killing it yourself, its promoting the sale of more meat. Remember, supply and demand.

Broccoli and Cheese

BROCCOLI AND CHEESE;

Cook two pounds of broccoli.
You can bring water to a boil in a large kettle and drop in your broccoli, boil for 3-5 minutes and drain.
Place the broccoli in a casserole dish.

In another saucepan add:
3 cups of soy milk
and 1 pound of Velveta Cheese cut into cubes
heat slowly and stir until cheese melts
pour this mixture over the cooked broccoli
salt and pepper

crush Ritz crackers, I use two tubes or ¾ of a box
spread the crushed crackers on top of the broccoli and cheese

bake for about 35 minutes 325 until top lightly browns

Zucchini and Summer Squash

ZUCCHINI AND SUMMER SQUASH:

Buy six medium summer and zucchini squash.
Slice them about ½ inch thick as pictured:

in a large kettle melt 1 stick of butter
then add the sliced squash
salt and pepper
cook over medium heat stirring until almost tender.
Serve

Banana nut cake

BANANA NUT CAKE:

Mix:
1 cup Crisco shortening
3 cups sugar
then add 4 eggs one at a time slowly:
Next add 4 cups flour
1/2 tsp. baking powder
1/2 tsp. baking soda, 1/2 tsp. salt
2 cups ripe bananas (mashed)
1/2 cup soy or almond milk
1tsp. Vanilla, 1 cup chopped pecans

Bake 350 for 50 to 60 minutes in a loaf pan

Banana cake icing:
2 cups sugar, 2 tbs. cornstarch
1/2 cup soy or almond milk
1/2 stick margarine
1 cup chopped pecan

Combine all in a saucepan and bring to rapid boil and remove from heat and add 1 tsp. vanilla. then beat until ready to pour over cake.

Halloween Pumpkin Spice Cupcakes

HALLOWEEN PUMPKIN SPICE CUPCAKES:

Mix in a large bowl:

1 Spice Cake Mix
follow the directions on the package

Then mix in 1 can (15 0z.) pumpkin
Mix well.

Put papers in your cupcake tins and fill ½ full
Bake 350 degree oven until done
Cool, frost and decorate

CHAPTER SIXTEEN: LYAWATA SCHNEIDER

Squash Casserole

1 medium butternut squash peeled and cut in small
pieces. Cook till tender and mash.
1 sweet red pepper chopped,1 or 2 small onions chopped
1 tablespoon olive oil
1 cup of fresh, frozen, or canned corn
3/4 lb. Monterey Jack cheese shredded
1 egg

Directions:
Cook Squash and mash.
Sauté pepper, onions, in olive oil.
Add egg and sautéed mix to squash. Add corn and cheese.
Save some of the cheese to put on top of casserole.
Bake at 350 for 40 minutes.
Serve with salsa on side.

BLUE CORN AND AMARANTH PANCAKES:

Mix together:
1 1/4 cup blue corn meal
1 1/4 cup amaranth flour
1 1/2 tsps. baking powder
1cup of milk
2 large eggs
2 tablespoons oil

Mix and cook on griddle. Serve with fruit and/or syrup.

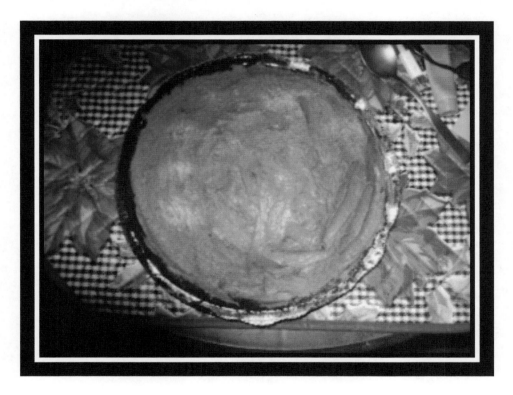

No bake Chocolate Cheesecake

1 1/2 cups semisweet chocolate chips
1 8 oz. plus 3 oz. cream cheese softened
1/2 cup sugar
1/4 cup butter softened
2 cups frozen whipped topping
1 8oz chocolate pie crust
Melt chips in microwave, stir until smooth

In medium bowl beat cream cheese, suga,and butter
together for 2 to 3 minutes with mixer

Stir in melted chocolate chips. fold in whipped
topping. Spoon mixture into a pie crust.
Refrigerate until serving. Nice to use a little extra
topping on the cheesecake! A very rich
Desert for chocolate lovers.

beans and franks

Easy hors d'ovares!

2 packages of Small Veggie Dogs or similar
2 cups catsup
2 cans jellied cranberry sauce
Dash of Tabasco
Cook Veggie dogs and sauce together until well mixed.
Serve with toothpicks, and a side of Tabasco sauce.

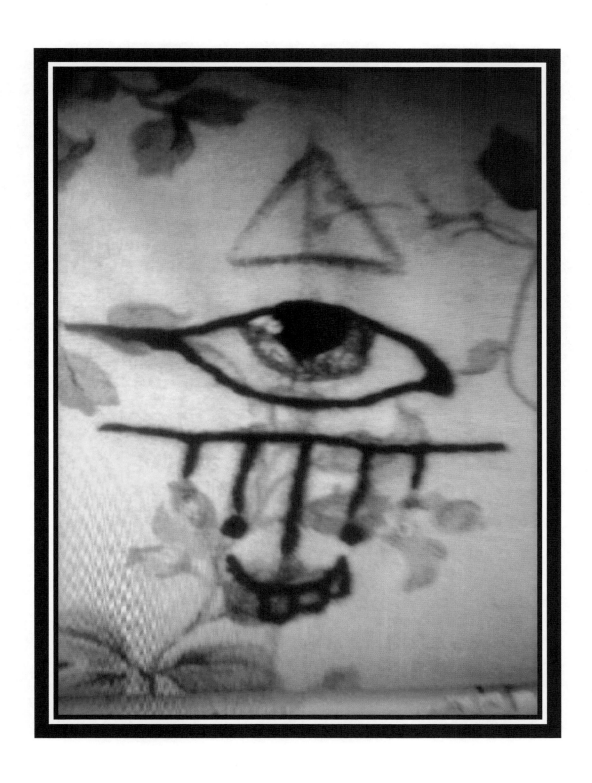

Caesar Salad

CAESAR SALAD:

Mix in a large bowl:

1 head of Romain lettuce
½ cup of shredded carrot
3 tab. Parmesan Cheese
2 small cucumbers peeled and chopped

Lightly mix it together

Serve with croutons and creamy Caesar Dressing.

Vegetables and shrimp with Marinade stir-fry

MARINADE: Stir Fry
(sweet and tangy)

Mix in a small bowl:

¼ cup of lime and lemon juice
1 tab. vinegar
a dash of salt and pepper
¼ cup chopped chives
¼ cup olive oil
½ tsp. oregano
½ cup fresh chopped basil
1 tab. sugar
2 tab. curry of your choice
2 tab. soy sauce

in the photo the vegetables used were:
summer squash, broccoli rabe, and onions

use this marinade for a tasty stir-fry
serve over rice.

STIR FRY:

in a frying pan:
add ¼ cup olive oil
add your choice of vegetables and shrimp or both.

Sauté with marinade until done.

Homemade Banana Bread

HOMEMADE BANANA BREAD:

Mix in a bowl:
1 ½ cups sugar
1 ½ tsp. baking powder
1 tsp. salt.
1 ½ tsp. cinnamon
¾ tsp. cloves
2/3 cup shortening
2/3 cup soy milk
3 eggs

mix with mixer
Then add 3 mashed bananas
Mix again with mixer
Add 2 ¾ cup flour
If mixture seems too thick add a little more soy milk so you get a nice
batter.

Pour batter into bread pans about half way full
Bake 45-60 minutes
Stick toothpick into center to see if they are done

Top with Walnuts
Or you can also make a banana cake using this same
recipe. Just cook it in a large cake pan
Cook and frost with Buttercream Frosting

Curried Vegetables

CURRIED VEGETABLES:

Prepare the vegetables:
Slice up about 3 cups of green zucchini and yellow summer squash
Dice 1 cup of shallots
1 cup of cubed potatoes
1 cup cubed red and yellow sweet peppers
cook in about 2 tablespoons olive oil until vegetables are tender.
Add 1 jar of Pataks Yellow Korma Curry
A dash of cumin and a dash of cayenne pepper
1 can of chunk pineapple
cook ten minutes or so until hot and bubbly.

Serve over hot steamed jasmine rice

Personal Notes and Recipes:

Chocolate Mousse Cheese Pie

CHEESE CHOCOLATE MOUSSE PIE:

Melt a 12 ounce package chocolate chips and cool. (if you put the chips in a small saucepan, and then put that pan over a bigger pan filled ½ full of water, and heat, it will melt the chocolate without burning it)

In a bowl blend:
1 8 oz. package cream cheese
½ tsp. salt, 1 tsp. vanilla
Then beat in:
Melted chocolate and blend well.

Buy 1 prepared crust
Melt 12 0z. package semi-sweet chocolate

In a separate bowl:

Beat the 2 egg whites until stiff adding ¼ cup sugar as you beat them.
Beat until stiff and glossy. Fold into chocolate mixture.

In a separate bowl:

Whip one cup of heavy cream adding 3 tab. sugar and 2 tsp. vanilla as you beat it. (beat until nice and thick) (you could use cool whip instead of heavy cream)
Save about ¼ of the mixture for the topping
And fold into chocolate mixture.
Pour into your crust.
And top with the extra whipped cream
Chill until filling sets.

If you would like to make LEMON CHEESE CAKE instead,
Substitute the melted chocolate for 1 1/8 tsp. Lemon extract.

CHEESECAKE:
Mix together:

1 pound cream cheese. 1 tsp. vanilla, ¾ cup of sugar, 2 eggs,
pour mixture in a prepared graham cracker curst and bake at 350 degrees 25 minutes/ top with cool whip or fruit when cooled.

Jelly Pancakes

JELLY PANCAKES;

Beat 3 eggs and add 1 tsp. sugar
½ tsp. salt
1 cup milk
and mix until smooth
add 1 cup flour.
Make sure the mixture is thin.
Pour by ladle onto a hot greased frying pan and cook until bottom is browned and
flip over.
Pancakes should be thin, if not add more milk, if mixture is too thin add more
flour.   Spread jelly on each pancake and roll up

Personal Notes and Recipes:

Congo Bars

CONGO BARS:

Use one large greased cookie sheet
Mix:
2 tsp. baking soda
2 tsp. salt, 4 sticks butter
1 ½ cup sugar
1 ½ cup brown sugar
2 tsp. vanilla
4 eggs
then: after mixing add 1 large package chocolate chips (two if you want more chocolate)
1 cup walnuts (optional)
then stir in by hand 4-5 cups flour to make a cookie batter

spread the batter onto the cookie sheet and bake 325 degrees 30 minutes
cool and cut into squares
You can use this same recipe to make Chocolate Chip Cookies

CHAPTER EIGHTEEN: THE HEALTH BENEFITS OF SAURERKRAUT

(sauerkraut and cabbage)

Sauerkraut combines the health benefits offered by all cruciferous vegetables (a category which includes cauliflowers and brussel sprouts as well as cabbage) with the probiotic advantages derived from the fermentation process.

Cabbage offers a host of health benefits. It is high in vitamins A and C. Studies have shown the cruciferous vegetables can help lower cholesterol levels. Cabbage also provides a rich source of phytonutrient antioxidants. In addition, it has anti-inflammatory properties, and some studies indicate it may help combat some cancers. However, this already helpful vegetable becomes a super food when it is pickled.

The fermentation process used to make sauerkraut was probably first developed centuries ago simply as a means of preserving vegetables for easy consumption throughout the winter. The health benefits derived from pickling vegetables were already well known to early civilizations. Historical evidence suggests laborers on the Great Wall of China consumed a version of the pickled cabbage dish 2,000 years ago.

Traditional Chinese has long prescribed sauerkraut juice as a home remedy for many common ailments. The armies of Genghis Khan most likely first brought the dish to Europe. The Roman army traveled with barrels of sauerkraut, using it to prevent intestinal infections among the troops during long excursions.

In periods and cultures when natural healing methods fell into disuse, people consumed fewer fermented foods and were subject to more illness. Scurvy (vitamin C deficiency) killed many British sailors during the 1700s, especially on longer voyages. In the late 1770s, Captain James Cook circumnavigated the world without losing a single sailor to scurvy, thanks to the foods his ship carried, including sixty barrels of sauerkraut.

Mainstream health experts began to pay renewed attention to sauerkraut after a study published in The Journal of Agricultural and Food Chemistry in 2002. Finnish researchers reported that in laboratory studies, a substance produced by fermented cabbage, isothiocyanates, helped prevent the growth of cancer.

Healthy human colons contain many beneficial bacteria which feed on the waste left over from our digestion, creating lactic acid. Without these beneficial bacteria the human digestive system becomes home to harmful parasites and yeasts, resulting in the condition of candida.

Sauerkraut provides a high density source of a wide range of beneficial live bacteria which assist in the digestive process. Consuming a serving of sauerkraut can give your body as much of a health boost as many of the expensive probiotic drinks and

supplements sold in stores. However, most commercially sold sauerkraut have lost most of their beneficial bacterial organisms. To gain the most benefits from sauerkraut, you may want to purchase it freshly made, or learn how to make your own.
If you want to explore recipes for making sauerkraut and other fermented dishes, an excellent place to start is with Sandor Ellis Katz's Wild Fermentation: The Flavor, Nutrition and Craft of Live Culture Foods.

SOME RECIPE IDEAS:

Purchase a bag of sauerkraut in the refrigerated section of the grocery store. (canned does not taste as good)

When you are ready to use it, put the sauerkraut in a strainer and rinse it well to remove excess salt.

Now you can store it in your refrigerator and use it as needed.

Try adding it to your scrambled eggs.
Heat some sauerkraut and add some butter and pepper as a side dish.
You can also add sausage to the sauerkraut (veggie sausage)
Or add some to your favorite soup recipe

Vegetable Lasagna

VEGGIE LASAGNA:
You will need:

1 green Zucchini (diced)
1 yellow squash (diced)
1 package of sliced mushroom
1 package of chopped spinach (frozen)
1 jar of spaghetti sauce of your choice
1 box of lasagna noodles

1 -16 oz. package of Ricotta Cheese
1 -16 oz. Mozzarella Cheese
Then sauté chopped vegetables until tender
Cook and drain chopped frozen spinach, cool
Then mix with the Ricotta Cheese
Cook lasagna noodles according to directions
Layer lasagna as follows:
Layer one-veggies with spinach Ricotta mixture
Layer two-red sauce and Mozzarella
Sauté chopped begetables until tender, cook and drain chopped
frozen spinach, cool then mix with ricotta cheese. Repeat steps.
Top with Mozzarella until mostly cover
Bake at 350 degrees for 40-50 minutes
Uncover and bake for an additional 10 minutes

KELSEY'S CHILI:

Combine:

2 cups textured vegetable protein moistened with warm water or
vegetable broth.

Add to your frying pan and add 2 tab. oil, 1 clove garlic chopped,
and1 medium onion chopped, stir and fry

Put in a large pot and add:2 cans (15 oz.) Kidney Beans, 2 cans (15
oz.) tomatoes, 1 tsp. Cumin. 2 tsp. chili powder, 1 tsp. salt, black
pepper to taste2 tsp. Worcestershire Sauce, 7 oz. canned hot salsa.
bring to a boil and reduce heat and simmer an hour

if you need more flavor add Chili Power if you need more heat add
Cumin

Muffin Eggs

MUFFIN EGGS:

Spray a muffin tin that holds 12 muffinsAdd one egg to each cup, whole or if you prefer whip the egg firstAdd spinach or whatever types of veggies you would like to use, you can precook the veggies or use them rawYou can also add shredded cheeseAdd salt and pepper, crushed red pepper and or garlic powder to taste. Mix with a fork to break the yolk and combineBake at 350 degrees for ten minutes being careful not to overcookSet aside to cool. You can also freeze these until ready to eat. In the morning toast an English muffin and while the muffin is toasting you can heat or microwave the frozen egg and make a muffin sandwich. Enjoy!

CHAPTER TWENTY: WHY GIVE UP DAIRY?

Dairy products are not a healthy choice for the human body. Dairy has a high saturated fat content. And the best reason of all is having happy cows. Do some research on the lives of a dairy cow. Did you know that to get milk, the cow has to be pregnant, so the cow is kept pregnant and when she gives birth her baby is taken away. If it's a male it will be sold to the veal industry, and a girl is kept for a future milk producer. Nothing is natural about this, its mean and cruel.

Cow milk is produced for baby cows, cat milk for baby kittens, dog milk for baby dogs. Dairy is not good for us, but the dairy industry does not want you to know that. We do not need dairy to make strong bones and teeth. Look at all of the large animals on our planet, for instance the elephant, its a vegetarian, has huge bones and tusks and does not eat dairy. We do not need dairy to be healthy, and lots of people would be healthier if they eliminated dairy from their diet.

One of the best ways to help animals is to eliminate dairy products. Today we have many other foods we can eat to replace our love of dairy products. And did you know that a cow can live to the age of twenty? but most are killed at the slaughter house before they turn five as their milk production is not as good as a younger cow. And did you realize cows love their babies. They cry and moo for weeks when after birth when the baby

cow is taken away. For more detailed information about the dairy industry's cruel farming practices, a great book to read: *Meat Market: Animals, Ethics, and Money* or Jonathan Safran Foer's *Eating Animals*.

Here are some dairy substitutions:

Butter: Earth Balance and Soy Garden are excellent vegan choices. I love Earth Balance and it tastes great on toast. I also use a product called "Melt" its a virgin coconut oil organic based spread, great on toast and vegetables.

Yogurt: You can now buy yogurt made from Soy or Coconut milk. Many choices are available. I find the soy yogurt a little getting use to, but its really tasty, and you can add fresh fruit to it. You can also use this to substitute for sour cream, just get plain soy yogurt.

Milk: Soy, rice, almond, flax and coconut milk is now available and they are much healthier for you to consume. Try them and find your favorite one. Some of them are flavored vanilla, and now you can even buy soy chocolate milk.

Cheese: There are many non-dairy cheeses on the market. Vegan cheeses are great, try different ones until you find your favorites.

Ice Cream: Turtle Mountain, Double Rainbow ,So Delicious and Tufutti make vegan ice cream. Also sorbets, just check the ingredients on the label.I have found all these brands at my local health food store. The coconut ice cream bar is out of this world. **Cream Cheese, Sour Cream, and Mayo:** You can find these products at your whole foods store or health food stores. Lots of food chains now carry vegan foods.

Coffee Creamer: there are many brands of non-dairy coffee creamers now on the market and in all flavors.

Two great books to read:

Vegan: The New Ethics Of Eating by Erik Marcus.

His other book called " The Ultimate Vegan Guide" Compassionate Living Without Sacrifice" covers everything from cooking, nutrition, food shopping, travel, dining out and much more.

Cashew Cheese is great for pizza, grilled cheese sandwiches or anything you like to use cheese on. It melts great and your going to love this. This recipe is found in the book: The Ultimate Vegan Guide.

A cow can show happiness!

check out this "you tube" video: "Happy Cows" you won't believe the reaction of these cows"

CHAPTER TWENTY-ONE: CADENCE

Hermit Cookies

HERMIT COOKIES;

Mix together:
1 cup vegetable oil
½ cup molasses
½ cut water
1 Tab. instant coffee
2 eggs
2 tsp. baking soda
2 tsp. cinnamon
2 tsp. cloves
1 tsp. salt
1 ½ cup raisins
4 ½ cups flour

Pre heat over 350 degrees
Dissolve instant coffee in water
Beat eggs and add in coffee mixture, oil and molasses and mix until well blended.
In a separate bowl mix together the sugar, baking soda, cinnamon, cloves and salt.
Add dry ingredients into wet. Mix well and add the raisins.
Spoon by the tablespoon onto a greased cookie sheet/or bake on a sheet and cut into squares
Bake until done

Gingerbread Cupcakes

Gingerbread Cupcakes

Mix together:

1 cup of molasses, 1 cup of water, ½ oleo,
1 egg, ½ tsp. salt, 1 tsp. baking soda,
1 tsp. ginger, 1 tsp. cinnamon, 1 cup sugar
mix well then mix in 3 cups of flour

spray muffin tins and fill ¾ full with batter
bake at 350 degrees 20-25 minutes

Cream Cheese Frosting

Soften one package cream cheese
Mix with two sticks of oleo and add 1 tsp. vanilla
1 tsp. cinnamon, ½ tsp. nutmeg and two cups of
powdered sugar.
cream together.
Frost cupcakes when cool

Apple Pie Filling

Preparing the Filling

APPLE PIE:

Preheat over to 350 degrees

CRUST:
2 ½ cups flour, 1 tsp. salt, 3 sticks of oleo softened to room temp.
6 tabs. water,
in a medium bowl mix together the flour and salt.
Cut in the oleo and cream together until smooth.
Sprinkle with water and stir with a fork until moistened.
With your hands, gather up the dough and divide into two

Equal parts. Roll out each section on a floured surface to fit your pie plate.

PIE FILLING:

1 cup of sugar, 2 tabs. flour, 1 tsp. cinnamon, ½ tsp. nutmeg, ¼ tsp. salt and 7 apples

peel and core and chop the apples to bite sized pieces
in a large bowl mix together the flour, sugar, salt, cinnamon and nutmeg.
Toss in apples and mix until coated.
Line pie plate with half of the rolled out pie crust. Poke with a fork a few times and add apple mixture and top with the remaining rolled out pie crust.
Use a fork to seal edges of pie crust. Make a small "x" in the center of the crust.
Brush top of pie crust with a beaten egg and sprinkle with sugar
Bake 350 degrees for 40-50 minutes

Tomato Sauce

TOMATO SAUCE:

5 pounds of tomatoes, 1 bulb of garlic, a handful of basil (about 10-12 leaves) 1 yellow onion, 1 package of baby bella mushrooms, sliced, ½ cup grated parmesan cheese, 6 oz. can tomato paste, 1 tabs. salt, 1 tsp. pepper, 1/2 tsp. paprika in a large baking pan arrange rough chopped tomatoes, onions, mushrooms and peeled garlic and herbs. Sprinkle with salt and pepper, paprika and cheese. Bake 350 degrees for 2-3 hours. Cover for the first hour with foil, stir once or twice during cooking. Remove herbs and transfer to a large pot and mix until smooth. (cool and then use a blender and blend until smooth.)

Now your ready to use your tomato sauce.

Before Baking

After Baking

Curried Eggplant

Curried Eggplant:

1 tabs. flour, 2 tabs. olive oil, 2 tabs. oleo, 1 large onion, chopped1 eggplant peeled and chopped into 1 inch cubes

3 tsp. curry powder, ½ tsp. ground ginger, 2 tabs. brown sugar,2 tabs. lemon juice, 1 ½ cup vegetable stock, 1 ½ tsp. salt,

½ tsp. pepper.

On med-low heat in a large saucepan soften onion in oil.

Push onion to outer rim of pan and melt oleo in the middle.

Sprinkle flour on melted oleo, cook butter and flour a few minutes and stir in the onions.

Turn up heat to high to med-high and add eggplant to pan and toss mixture. Cook stirring for a few minutes.

Add the lemon juice and spices turn down heat and cover, cook for 15-20 minutes stirring occasionally. Serve with steamed rice

Personal Notes and Recipes:

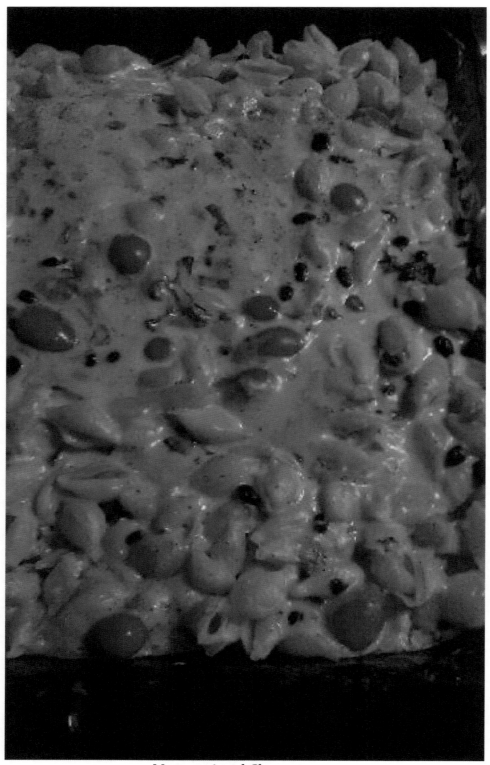

Macaroni and Cheese

MACARONI AND CHEESE:

In a large kettle cook one box of pasta shells, par cook and strain and set aside. In a large saucepan, caramelize 1 chopped onion and 2 tabs. of oleo. When the onions are soft and browned add 2 tabs. of flour and stir and cook for a couple of minutes.

Add 1 jalapeno pepper finely chopped and 1 habanero pepper finely chopped. Cook for a few minutes.

Whisk in 2 cups of almond milk and heat until almost to a boil, add in 1 pound of cubed cheddar cheese or Velveta cheese, and stir until cheese is melted. Salt and pepper to taste.

In a large casserole dish put the pasta and add one can of drained black beans.

Pour hot cheese mixture over the top.
Stir in 1 cups of cherry tomatoes and ½ cup of cilantro.
Bake at 350 degrees until bubble for about 15-20 minutes.

Stuffed Peppers

STUFFED PEPPERS;
You will need four large peppers:

Take the four large peppers and cut the tops off of the peppers and take out the seed/set aside

In your baking dish, grease and put a little tomato sauce on the bottom, place peppers in bake them for 15 minutes at 350 degrees

In a saucepan melt 2 tablespoons of oleo and add 1/2 cup onions and cook until they begin to caramelize.
Then stir in finely chopped left over pepper tops, 1/2 cup chopped baby bella mushrooms, 3 grated carrots and 7 cloves garlic, peeled and minced.

add 1/2 tsp. cayenne, 1 tsp. paprika , 1 tsp. ground chipotle cover and cook stirring for 6-8 minutes until vegetables are soft.
stir in rice and cook about 5 minutes longer, stirring occasionally.

Add one cup of vegetable stock, be sure to scrape bottom of pan to loosen any dripping and spices stuck to the bottom.

Stir in 1 cup of tomato sauce and cook another five minutes.

Spoon mixture into par cooked peppers
Top with 1/2 cup vegan parmesan cheese (optional)
bake peppers for 20 minutes at 350 degrees.

 By eating less meat we are really making a difference. It shows that we understand what is going on with factory farming and the cruelty it involves, so yes, by eating less meat, you are making a big difference!
And someday, you have to give something back to the animals. Let it be compassion, and freedom.

Homemade Coleslaw

HOMEMADE COLESLAW:

1 Large cabbage sliced
1 small purple cabbage sliced, 1 large carrot sliced
1 green pepper shredded, 1 medium onion sliced
1 cup olive oil (filippo berio brand)
3 tabs. sugar
1 cup garlic flavored wine vinegar, Cento brand
salt and pepper to taste

in a large mixing bowl combine the cabbage, carrots, peppers and onions.
In a separate bowl mix the oil, wine vinegar and sugar
Pour the dressing over the cabbage mixture. Toss well.
Cover and refrigerate until ready to use. Serves 6-8

Wine Biscuits

WINE BISCUITS:

1 cup of sugar
1 cup of oil
1 cup of wine (Lambrusco Riunite)
½ tsp. salt, 1 tsp. baking powder
4-5 cups of flour, 3 eggs, beaten

In a large mixing bowl, combine sugar, oil, wine and salt.
Mix well. Add baking power and flour to wet ilngredients
Keep adding enough flour until the mixture does not stick to you
hands while mixing.
Take small amounts of the dough and roll between your hands into a
rope about 4-5 inches long.
Leave the dough thicker in the center of the rope.
Preheat over to 350 degrees
Place on a cookie sheet, folding small ends under each other.
Fill the cookie sheet and brush biscuits with the beaten egg.
Cook in oven for about 20-25 minutes until golden brown.

Hint: biscuits only expand slightly during the cooking process.
Do not over cook
Remove from cookie sheet within 3-5 minutes
Yields about 50-55 biscuits

CHAPTER TWENTY-THREE: SO WHAT DO FACORY RAISED

FARM ANIMALS EAT? IN OTHER WORDS YOU EAT WHAT THEY EAT. "Source: unionofconcernedscientists.org

They Eat What?

The Reality of Feed at Animal Factories

When many Americans think of farm animals, they picture cattle munching grass on rolling pastures, chickens pecking on the ground outside of picturesque red barns, and pigs gobbling down food at the trough.

Over the last 50 years, the way food animals are raised and fed has changed dramatically—to the detriment of both animals and humans. Many people are surprised to find that most of the food animals in the United States are no longer raised on farms at all. Instead they come from crowded animal factories, also known as large confined animal feeding operations (CAFOs).

Just like other factories, animal factories are constantly searching for ways to shave their costs. To save money, they've redefined what constitutes animal feed, with little consideration of what is best for the animals or for human health. As a result, many of the ingredients used in feed these days are not the kind of food the animals are designed by nature to eat. Just take a look at what's being fed to the animals you eat. Same species meats, diseased animals, feathers, hair, skin, hooves, blood, manure and other animal waste, plastics, drugs and chemical, and unhealthy amounts of grains.

Are these ingredients legal? Unfortunately, yes. Nevertheless, some raise human health concerns. Others just indicate the low standards for animal feeds. But all are symptoms of a system that has lost sight of the appropriate way to raise food animals. **Same Species Meat, Diseased Animals, and Feathers, Hair, Skin, and Blood**

The advent of "mad cow" disease (also known as bovine spongiform encephalopathy or BSE) raised international concern about the safety of feeding rendered[1] cattle to cattle. Since the discovery of mad cow disease in the United States, the federal government has taken some action to restrict the parts of cattle that can be fed back to cattle. However, most animals are still allowed to eat meat from their own species. Pig carcasses can be rendered and fed back to pigs, chicken carcasses can be rendered and fed back to chickens, and turkey carcasses can be rendered and fed back to turkeys. Even cattle can still be fed cow blood and some other cow parts.Under current law, pigs, chickens, and turkeys that have been fed rendered cattle can be rendered and fed back to cattle—a loophole that may allow mad cow agents to infect healthy cattle.Animal feed legally can contain rendered road kill, dead horses, and euthanized cats and dogs. Rendered feathers, hair, skin, hooves, blood, and intestines can also be found in feed, often under catch-all categories like "animal protein products."**Manure and Other Animal Waste** Feed for any food animal can contain cattle manure, swine waste, and poultry litter. This waste may contain drugs such as antibiotics and hormones that have passed unchanged through the animals' bodies. The poultry litter that is fed to cattle contains rendered cattle parts in the form of digested poultry feed and spilled poultry feed. This is another loophole that may allow mad cow agents to infect healthy cattle.Animal waste used for feed is also allowed to contain dirt, rocks, sand, wood, and other such contaminants. **Plastics** :Many animals need roughage to move food through their digestive systems. But instead of using plant-based roughage, animal factories often turn to pellets made from plastics to compensate for the lack of natural fiber in the factory feed.

Drugs and Chemicals

Animals raised in humane conditions with appropriate space and food rarely require medical treatment. But animals at animal factories often receive antibiotics to promote faster growth and to compensate for crowded, stressful, and unsanitary living conditions. An estimated 13.5 million pounds of antibiotics—the same classes of antibiotics used in human medicine—are routinely added to animal feed or water. This routine, nontherapeutic use of antibiotics speeds the development of antibiotic-resistant bacteria, which can infect humans as well as animals. Antibiotic resistance is a pressing public health problem that costs the U.S. economy billions of dollars each year. Some of the antimicrobials used to control parasites and promote growth in poultry contain arsenic, a known human carcinogen. Arsenic can be found in meat or can contaminate human water supplies through runoff from factory farms.

Unhealthy Amounts of Grains

One last surprise. While grain may sound like a healthful food, the excessive quantities fed to some animals are not. This is especially true for cattle, which are natural grass eaters. Their digestive systems are not designed to handle the large amounts of corn they receive at feedlots. As a result of this corn-rich diet, feedlot cattle can suffer significant health problems, including excessively acidic digestive systems and liver abscesses. Grain-induced health problems, in turn, ramp up the

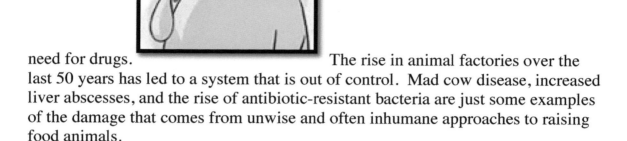

need for drugs. The rise in animal factories over the last 50 years has led to a system that is out of control. Mad cow disease, increased liver abscesses, and the rise of antibiotic-resistant bacteria are just some examples of the damage that comes from unwise and often inhumane approaches to raising food animals.

As a consumer armed with information, you have the power to promote a modern approach to raising animals that is both productive and healthful. You can help to effect change by supporting systems and producers that feed animals the food they were meant to eat.

You can:

- Avoid factory farmed animal products altogether by choosing plant-based foods.
- If you are going to eat any meat at least choose grass-fed and grass-finished beef and dairy products and pasture-raised pork, poultry, and egg products.
- Select certified organic meats, eggs, and dairy and those clearly labeled as using only vegetarian animal feed.

Coconut milk tofu chowder

COCONUT MILK TOFU CHOWDER:
Heat in a saucepan some olive oil and add 1 onion chopped and 2 toes of garlic, minced. sauté until tender.
One package of firm tofu and cube it. sauté with onions and garlic and add 1 tablespoon of soy sauce. Set aside.

In a large kettle add 2 cups of coconut milk, 1 tablespoon of oleo.
In a separate saucepan, sauté your choice of vegetables. Try beans, carrots, mushrooms, or cubed potatoes. The choice is yours.

Once the vegetables are done, add them to the coconut milk, add the onions and garlic and tofu. Stir in 1 tablespoon yellow curry, 2 tablespoons light brown sugar. Heat and serve.

Tomato Spinach Pizza

HOMEMADE TOMATO SPINACH PIZZA:

Buy the prepared pizza dough from your local bakery or supermarket.
It comes either fresh or frozen. If its frozen just let it thaw out. once your dough is ready, take a large cookie sheet and grease it with Crisco shortening. Place the dough in the middle of the pan and stretch it out until it's about ¼ inch thick.
Place the toppings on the pizza dough in this order:

Top with pizza sauce. Mozzarella cheese
Drained cooked spinach. Fresh sliced tomatoes
Sprinkle with fresh basil, salt and pepper

Bake 375 degrees oven until bottom crust is browned

Oatmeal Blueberry Health Cookies

OATMEAL BLUEBERRY HEALTH COOKIES:

In a large bowl combine:

1 cup oleo
1 cup brown sugar
1 cup sugar
2 tablespoons vanilla
1 teaspoon baking soda
1 teaspoon salt

In a blender mix:

4 eggs. 1 carrot, 1 cup cranberries.
Blend and add to bowl, then with a mixer mix contents of bowl.
Add one cup of fresh blueberries (or frozen) and mix again with a spoon
Add 3 cups of oatmeal, 2 cups of flour and mix

Drop by spoonful onto cookie sheet and bake 325 degrees until done
About 15-20 minutes

Broccoli or Spinach Quiche

BROCCOLI OR SPINACH QUICHE:

Sauté ½ cup chopped onion and set aside
Mix in a bowl:
4 beaten eggs
2 cups light cream
¾ tsp. salt, ½ tsp pepper

make a pie crust for the bottom of a pie plate, or you can just grease
the bottom of pie plate and make the Quiche without a crust.
In the bottom, place you cooked chopped broccoli (2 cups) or 1
package of spinach cooked and drained. (you can use any
vegetables you like)
1 package vegan shredded cheese
Add the onions and pour in the egg mixture.
Bake 400 degrees 35-40 minutes.
Cook until the top browns and puffs.

Barley Mulligan Stew

BARLEY MULLIGAN STEW:

Soak ¾ cup barley for two hours.
Moisten 2 cups Textured Vegetable Protein with stock
Then sauté:
1 green pepper chopped
1 onion chopped, 1 clove garlic minced
Put all of the above in a large kettle and add:
1 large can tomatoes
1 can tomato paste, 2 cups water
1 tab. Vegan Beef or vegetable bouillon
2 tsp. salt
½ tsp. pepper
1 tab. Brown sugar
1 tab. Vinegar
Heat to a boil, reduce heat and cover and simmer 1 hour

Fresh Grilled Squash

FRESH GRILLED SQUASH:

Buy some fresh Summer and Green Squash, cut lengthwise
and place on a sheet of heavy duty foil.
Salt and pepper and put a few dabs of butter on top of the squash.
Wrap tightly and place on your grill. It should take about 10 minutes
for the squash to cook. Open and serve.

Stuffed Pepper with Shitake Mushrooms

STUFFED PEPPER WITH SHITAKE MUSHROOMS:

Buy and cut in half four large red and green peppers
Cut in half and remove the seeds. Set aside.

Mix 3 cups of cooked cooled rice with 2 cups Textured Vegetable
Protein that has been moistened with stock.
Add 2 cloves garlic chopped and 1 cup of chopped onions,
2 eggs, 1 tsp. salt and 1 tsp. pepper. 1 tab. parsley, 1 tab. basil
mix well and stuff the pepper halves.
Place in a greased baking pan.
Top each stuffed pepper with your favorite tomato sauce and top
each one with a Shitake Mushroom (precook mushrooms in olive oil)
Cover with foil and bake 40 minutes 350 degrees.

(you can purchase fresh or dried Shitake Mushrooms/if you purchase
the dried ones, just soak them in warm water until soft)

Fresh Garden Salad

FRESH GARDEN SALAD:

Prepare for salad:
Romaine Lettuce,
Tomato, Cucumber,Green Pepper
Arrange in bowl
Add 1 tablespoon Humas
1 tablespoon Chick Peas
1 tablespoon Avacado
add some Falafel
top with grated cheese
serve with your favorite salad dressing

Stuffed Portobello Mushroom

STUFFED PORTOBELLO MUSHROOM

Purchase 6 large Portobello mushrooms
Remove the stems. Chop the stems up and sauté with ¼ cup of
grape seed oil or olive oil
And add: 1 chopped yellow pepper, 1 chopped sweet onion
3 cloves of garlic, diced, 1 chopped fresh tomato
sauté a few minutes and add in one package of fresh spinach
cook until spinach is tender.
Now fill the caps with the filling and cover each cap with about 1
tablespoon of Feta cheese and 1 slice of fresh tomato
Bake for ½ hour at 400 degrees
When the mushrooms are done, cover the tops with fresh chopped
Avocado and drizzle with balsamic vinegar.

Double Bran Banana Muffins

LISA'S DOUBLE BRAN BANANA MUFFINS

Mix in a large bowl:
2 cups whole wheat flour
½ cup wheat bran
½ cup oat bran
½ cup oats
1 ½ tsp. baking soda
½ tsp. sea salt
mix lightly, then add:

2 cups vanilla yogurt
1/3 and a bit cup of honey
¼ cup oil, 1-2 tsp. vanilla extract
In the blender put in two large bananas and two eggs
Blend and add to bowl
mix well
then add and mix in:
1 cup raisins or
berries optional

Bake 375 degrees 15 minutes

Personal Notes and Recipes:

BRAN FLAX MUFFINS:

In a large bowl mix:
2 cups white unbleached flour
¾ cup flax seed meal
¾ cup oat bran
1 ¼ cup brown sugar
2 tsp. baking soda
1 tsp. baking powder
½ tsp. sea salt
2 tsp. cinnamon
1 cup of carrot shredded
3 apples peeled and diced
½ cup raisins
1 mashed banana
1 cup almond milk
3 eggs beaten
2 tsp. vanilla extract

mix well and fill greased muffin pans half full
bake 350 degrees about 20 minutes

Peanut Sauce

PEANUT SAUCE;

Heat oil in frying pan
Add:
½ cup chopped green onions
1 tab. chopped ginger
2 garlic cloves minced
cook and add:
1 cup coconut milk
½ cup vegetable broth
½ cup creamy peanut butter
2 tab. Asian Fish Sauce
2 tab. lime juice
½ tsp. salt
½ tsp. crushed red pepper

simmer 5 minutes stirring. Serve with your favorite food.
You can add 2 tsp. yellow curry or 2 tsp. yellow curry paste if you want to make Curry Peanut Sauce.

This sauce is great added to noodles or on top of Fried Tofu as pictured.

Fried Tofu with Peanut Sauce

Dilly Bread

DILLY BREAD:

Mix one package dry yeast with ¼ cup luke warm water
Then add to that:
1 cup vegan cream cheese (room temperature)
2 tab. sugar
1 tab. butter
2 tsp. dill seed,1 tsp. sea salt
½ tsp. baking soda. 2 eggs beaten
and stir well
then add:
2 ¼ cups flour
knead and cover and let it rise one hour
knock it down and put it in a casserole dish and let it rise again.
Then bake 350 degrees for 45 minutes

Its great sliced warm with butter
and served with homemade soup.

Peanut Butter Cookies

PEANUT BUTTER COOKIES:

Mix in a bowl:
1 tab. vanilla
½ tsp. baking soda, ¼ tsp. salt
1 ¼ cup sugar, 1 ¼ cup brown sugar
1 cup oleo (2 sticks), 4 eggs
1 cup peanut butter (creamy or chunky)
blend well
stir in 4 – 5 cups flour until you have a nice batter.
Take about a tablespoon of batter and roll into a ball and place onto a greased cookie sheet.
Use a fort to press down each ball. flour the fork to prevent sticking.
Bake 325 degrees until done about 15-20 minutes

Rum Balls

RUM BALLS:

Mix in a bowl:

3 cups ground up vanilla wafers
1 cup ground walnuts
1 cup confectioners sugar
3 tab. corn syrup, 1 ½ tsp. cocoa
1/2 cup rum
mix and roll into balls
roll in confectioners sugar
store in a tight container

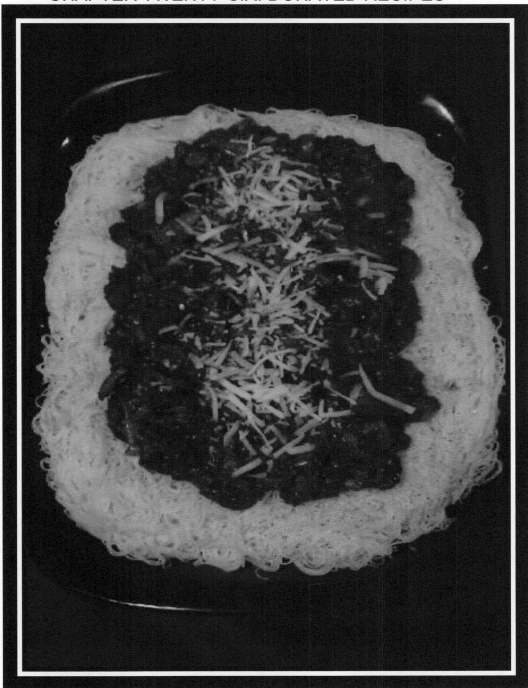

Eggplant Spaghetti Sauce

EGGPLANT SPAGHETTI SAUCE:
(President Jimmy Carter and Mrs. Rosalynn Carter)

1 eggplant, cut into cubes (peeled or unpeeled)
3 Tablespoons oil
1 onion, sliced
1 garlic clove, minced
1 green pepper, sliced
1 cup plum tomatoes
1 cup tomato juice
1 teaspoon oregano, 2 teaspoons basil

Saute eggplant in oil about 7 minutes, add onion, garlic and peppers, and sauté 3 additional minutes, or until tender.

Combine tomatoes, tomato juice and herbs. Add to the eggplant mixture.

Cover and simmer for about ½ hour. Serve over spaghetti

Vegetable and Potato Stew

VEGETABLE AND POTATO STEW:
(Corrine my friend from New Zealand)

3 Large potatoes cubes
1 onion sliced
5 celery stalks cut into large pieces
5 carrots cut into large pieces
1 red pepper cubed
1 green pepper cubed
6 fresh mushrooms sliced
a variety of fresh or frozen vegetables (green beans, corn, peas, zucchini, spinach, kale)
1 clove garlic minced
salt and pepper to taste, 4 cups of vegetable broth

place the ingredients in a large kettle or slow cooker.
Cook on low heat until done.
Then when done, sift 5 tablespoons of flour into kettle while stirring the vegetables. Let it simmer for 10 minutes. It will thicken
Serve in a bread bowl or over a thick slice of Italian bread.
It's very hearty!

Roasted Red Pepper Soup

ROASTED RED PEPPER SOUP:
(Linda Manning)

Makes about 4 cups

Bring 5 cups of water or stock to a boil and add 1/2 cup of lentils or beans of your choice
(if using lentils simmer for 45 minutes, if using canned beans you can just bring it to a boil and turn down the heat.
Then add 1 large can of diced tomatoes with the juice
1 jar of roasted red peppers chopped up
1 tablespoon of tomato paste, 1/2 cup of frozen corn. Heat and serve.

Rich and Awesome High Protein Balls

RICH AND AWESOME HIGH PROTEIN BALLS:
(Elizabeth Silva)

mix together:
1/2 cup chopped cashews, walnuts or almonds or a mixture of all three
1 scoop veggie protein powder
½ cup sesame seeds, ½ cup oatmeal
½ cup pumpkin seeds
mix together and add:
1 cup of peanut butter
2 Tbsp.honey
mix well, then dampen hands and form abut 1 inch size balls. Then roll each one in sesame seeds.
(keep in a container and refrigerate)
You can also freeze these for a quick snack anytime. Just let thaw a few minutes
(you can use whatever you like in the peanut butter mix)

Cranberry Fruit Squares

WONDERFUL FRUIT SQUARES
(Mary Ellen, Seekonk Library)

Mix in a large bowl:
3 sticks of butter
3 cups of sugar
4 eggs
1 tsp. salt
1 tsp. vanilla
1. tsp. baking powder
mix well and add either
4 cups cranberries or 4 cups of blueberries (fresh or frozen)
add 2 cups chopped walnuts
3 cups flour and mix together
Spread on a large greased cookie sheet
Bake 350 degrees about 25 minutes until done
Cool and sprinkle top with confectionary sugar

Caramel Walnut Bars

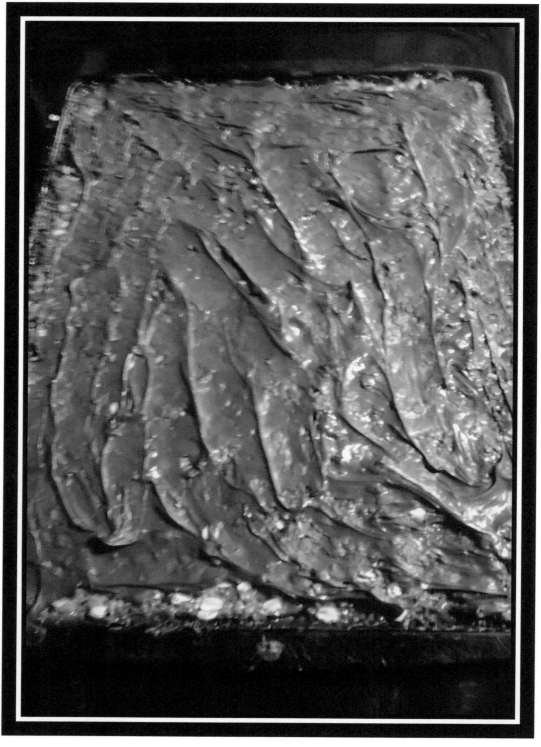

CARAMEL WALNUT BARS:
(a favorite from my friend Cathy)

Mix in a large bowl:
4 cups flour
1 ½ cup brown sugar
3 eggs
2 sticks butter
2 cups chopped walnuts
then press ¾ of the mixture onto your cookie sheet.
Save the rest for the topping

Mix 1 jar of caramel and 1 can condensed milk with ¼ cup of butter
and warm in a saucepan until butter melts
Pour this over the crust and top with the rest of the mixture.
You can also add oatmeal to the topping

Bake 350 degrees 25 minutes

(Optional) When done, remove from oven and pour one bag of
chocolate chips over the top. Let set a few minutes to melt and then
spread it with a spoon.

You can also use raspberry or lemon filling instead of the caramel,
but do not use the condensed milk if you do.

Rich Hot Rolls

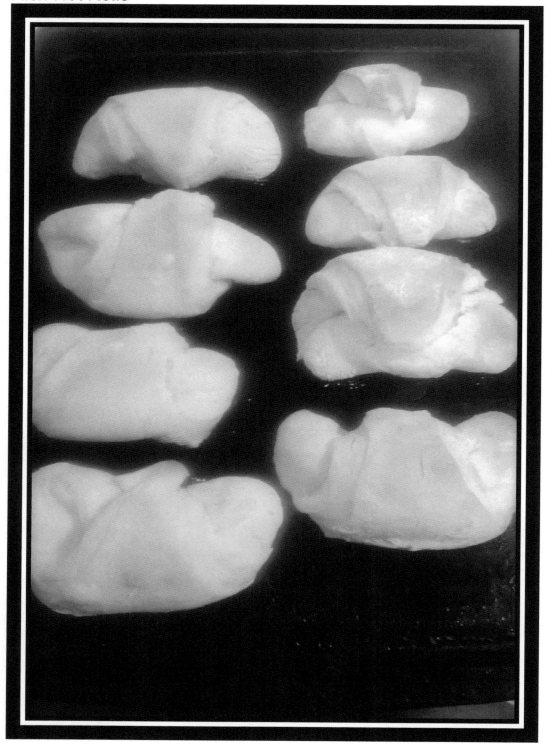

RICH HOT ROLLS:
(Grandma Bolton)

scald ¾ cup almond milk
add ½ cup shortening, ¾ cup sugar and 1 tsp. salt
cook to lukewarm, sprinkle 2 packages of dry yeast into 1/2 cup of
lukewarm water, stir to dissolve
then to the milk mixture add 1 ½ cups flour and beat well
then beat in yeast and 2 eggs
stir in enough flour to make a soft dough. Knead until smooth
place in a greased bowl and cover and let rise 1 ½ hours then punch
down and divide the dough in half

roll each half out like a pie crust/melt 2 tab. butter and spread on it
cut like a pizza and roll each pizza slice into crescents

place on a greased pan brush top with butter, let rise until double and
bake 350 degrees for about 10-15 minutes

jelly or jam is good on these too.

Cinnamon Rolls

CINNAMON ROLLS:
(Grandma Bolton)
Use the same dough for the Rich Hot Rolls
Divide the dough in half and roll out each half.

In a bowl mix:
1 cup sugar, 1 tab. cinnamon
1 tab. melted butter
then spread half of the mix on each half of the dough
you can add some raisins if you like

roll each like a jelly roll and seal the edges.
Cut in 1 inch slices and place on a greased cookie sheet. Cover and
let rise until double.
Bake 350 degrees about 20 minutes
Serve with butter or you can frost them too

PINEAPPLE UPSIDE DOWN CAKE:
(Jody Kingsley)

In a large bowl mix together with a electric mixer:
½ cup oleo, ¾ cup sugar, ½ cup soy or coconut milk,
1 tablespoon vanilla, and 2 eggs once blended, put mixture in a bowl
and stir in 2 cups of flour and mix until smooth.

Melt two tablespoons of oleo and put in the bottom of your baking
dish, then stir in ½ cup of brown sugar and mix.
Layer your pineapple rings on top of this mixture.
On top of this you can add 1 cup of crushed pecans or walnuts
Then pour your cake batter on top.
Bake 350 degrees 35 minutes or until done

Once the cake is cooled flip over
Great served with cool whip

Stuffed Dates

STUFFED DATES:
(Jody Kingsley)

Buy a package of pitted dates
Open each date and fill it with peanut butter
Then roll in powered sugar
And place a half of a walnut in the center of each one
Serve on a fancy dish

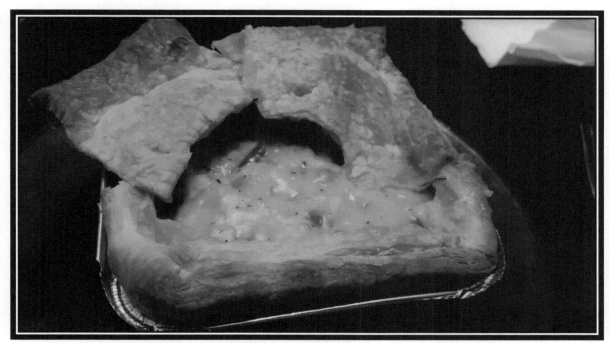

Savory Vegetable Pot Pie (vegan)

SAVORY VEGETABLE POT PIES: (Keith Burgeson)

Ingredients:
2 packages of frozen puff pastry sheets (Pepperidge farm brand)
1 cup plus 1 tablespoon vegan butter (earth balance brand)
1 cup flour, 6 cups vegan chicken or vegetable stock(better then
bouillon brand) 2 tablespoons oil, 1 tsp. sage, 1 tsp. thyme, pepper to
taste, 1 tablespoon nutritional yeast flakes, 1 tablespoon low-sodium
tamari soy sauce.

The use of meat-less chicken, such as Beyond Meat or Gardein brands are another option for the filling. Use fewer vegetables if these products are used.

Preparation:

Pre-heat oven to 375 degrees

Remove puff pastry from freezer to begin thawing.

Opening the package and separating/unfolding the pieces to help speed up the process. Each sheet has three segments.

To make the roux, melt the Earth Balance butter in a sauté pan, add flour and which constantly until light brown in color. Cool and set aside.

Bring six cups of water to a boil. Follow directions on chicken stock base for appropriate measurements.

In a large stockpot, cook frozen vegetables with vegetable oil until thawed and than add sage, thyme and pepper. Continue to cook for five minutes. Add already boiling stock. Whisk in nutritional yeast flakes and tamari. Add the roux a bit at a time and continue to cook as sauce begins to thicken. You may need to add some additional flour if the mixture does not thicken enough. Then pour the mixture into a large shallow pan to cool.

Grease the pot pie pans with butter, then line the bottom and sides of the pot pie pans with the thawed puff pastry.

Once the filling has cooled off, pour into individual pie dishes. Stretch the thawed puff pastry and use to cover the top of each one.

Take a knife and poke a few slits in the top of the pot pies to allow "breathing". Bake for 25-30 minutes or until the desired golden brown coloration is achieved.

Monkey Face Cookies

MONKEY FACE COOKIES:
(Grandma Bolton)

Mix in bowl:
1 egg, 1 cup sugar, ½ cup milk, ½ cup oleo, 1 tsp. vanilla and1 tsp. nutmeg and 2 cups flour.
once mixed, it will be like dough, which you can roll into balls and place on a greased cookie sheet, then flatten each one and put three raisins on each to make it look like a monkey face (eyes close together) bake 325 degrees until done

Pinwheel Cookies

PINWHEEL COOKIES: (Miriam Ruggles)
Mix:
1 ¼ cup butter, 1 ½ cup sugar, 1 egg, 3 cups flour, ½ tsp. salt,
1 tsp. vanilla, ½ cup milk
divide dough in half and add ½ cocoa and ½ cup sugar to half and
mix together
Chill dough one hour.
Then on a floured surface roll each out. place the dough with the
cocoa on top of the vanilla dough and roll up tightly. Chill again and
then slice about ½ inch thick
Place on a greased cookie sheet and bake 325 degrees ten minutes

Dark Chocolate Cranberry Avocado Cookies

DARK CHOCOLATE CRANBERRY AVOCADO COOKIES:
(Rev. Shari Johnson: Sacred Journeys)

These babies are very chocolaty with a little kick of spicy naughtiness. The Avocado replaces the butter and doesn't change the flavor.
Preheat over 350 degrees

In a food processor or blender combine ½ mashed avocado and ½ cup raw sugar or turbinado sugar.
Blend well.
Put in a bowl and add:
2 tsp. vanilla, 1 tsp. cidar vinegar,
½ tsp. baking powder, 2 tab. brewed coffee
2 tab. unsweetened cocoa powder
½ tsp. cayenne pepper, 2 tab. flaxseed meal
1 tsp. cinnamon
mix well
add in 1 cup flour any type
and mix until the batter is smooth.
Stir in 1 bag dark chocolate chips and ¾ cup dried cranberries
Add some chopped nuts if desired.

Spoon out about 1 tab. sized scoops of the dough and flatten into an even cookie like shape. (the dough will not spread when it bakes, so they will look like they do before they go into the oven)
Allow cookies to sit for 3 to 4 minutes before removing from cookie sheet.

Mock Cherry Pie

MOCK CHERRY PIE:
(Miriam B. Ruggles)

Makes enough pie dough for 2 pies.
Dough:
In a large bowl add 2 cups of flour
1 tsp. salt.
2 cups Crisco shortening, use a fork to blend together well.
Then add about 1 cup or so ice cold water.
Keep blending with the fork until the a dough forms but not sticky
Form into a loaf and cut into 4 equal sections.

Take a oven safe dinner plate (the secret to a good pie, is that you make it thin)

Roll one section of dough out to fit over the plate.
You will put ½ of the prepared filling on the dough, and cover it with another section of dough that you roll out.
Once the top is on, use a floured fork and fork the edges to seal.
Draw a little design in the middle of the pie dough top and bake at 325 degrees until browned.
Repeat for the other pie. You can bake both at the same time.

To prepare the filling:
Put in your blender:

2 cups of fresh cranberries (or frozen)
1 cup of raisins, 1 cup of water
2 tsp. vanilla
and blend

pour this mixture into a kettle and add 2 cups of sugar and two tsp. flour and stir and bring to a boil.
Now you can put this on the prepared pie crust cover and bake as directed.

Mock Cherry filling on prepared piecrust before covering

Coconut Pound Cake

COCONUT POUND CAKE:
(Ella Cranfield)

Cream:
1 ½ cup vegetable shortening
2 ½ cup sugar
5 eggs
beat for five minutes on high speed
then add:
3 cups flour
1 cup milk
1 tsp. baking powder, ¼ tsp. salt
beat again then mix in by hand:
7 oz. shredded coconut
2 tsp. coconut flavoring
½ tsp. lemon flavor

bake in a greased and floured angel tube pan for
1 hour 25 minutes 325 degrees until knife inserted comes out clean
cool cake before removing it from the pan.
This cake dries out easily and should be kept under cover to retain
moisture/ frost and serve

My grandmother was kidnapped when she was five years old, taken
from Tennessee to live in Northfield, Massachusetts.
She rode in the very first car that came to the Northfield Inn, when
she was a little girl.
When my grandmother was in her seventies, we got in touch with a
cousin from Tennessee and my mom and I drove there, to meet her
family for the first time.
This recipe was from a cousin we went to visit, in a log cabin in the
mountains of Tennessee. A wonderful cake never to be forgotten!

Butternut Squash

BUTTERNUT SQUASH:
(Tanya McIntyre)

Preheat over to 400 degrees
Cut butternut squash lengthwise
Scrape out seeds and place squash on a cookie sheet
Put pieces of butter in the scooped out "bowl" and also along
The flat length which I score with a knife so the butter does not just slide off.
Then add brown sugar to the same places.

Bake for about 1 hour or until a knife poked into the squash comes out easily

Once done, let it cool and the scrape out all the squash into a deep casserole dish.

Then add a few more pats of butter, some more brown sugar (about ¼ cup or more) salt, pepper and some cinnamon to taste.

(the amounts all depend on how much squash you cook)

Fork mash the squash until it not too lumpy but not completely smooth. Heat and serve

Rum Cake

RUM CAKE:
(Todd Tutcotte)
Mix in a large bowl:

1 cup chopped walnuts
1 yellow cake mix, 1 package instant vanilla pudding

4 eggs
½ cup milk
½ cup oil
½ cup Barcardi Dark Rum

once mixed pour batter into a Bundt Pan and bake 350 degrees 45 minutes until done
Cool. Then invert and prick the top with a fork

You can pour the rum directly onto the cooled cake or make a glaze
Or both.
Make your glaze:
 ½ cup butter melt and stir in:
1 cup sugar
1/4 cup water
and boil 5 minutes and remove from heat cool and stir in:

1/2 cup rum

then drizzle this glaze over cooled cake top.
This cake is amazing!

Lima Bean Soup

LIMA BEAN SOUP: (Evanne M. Mirabile)

Soak 1 pound dried baby lima bean overnight in cold water.
Drain and rinse.
Heat 3 tablespoons olive oil over medium heat.
Add 1 medium onion chopped and sauté until translucent for about
ten minutes Add:
1 14 ½ oz can of petite diced tomatoes
1 tablespoon dried oregano, 4 cups of water
1 teaspoon salt, ¼ teaspoon pepper
stir and simmer over low heat until beans are tender and broth has
thickened, for approximately 4 hours.

Romanian Gypsy Candy

ROMANIAN GYPSY CANDY:
(Michael and Andrada Draven)

Boil 6 good sized potatoes (do not peel) cook until done.
Cool and peel off the skin
Place in a bowl and mash them until there are no lumps
Add a ¼ cup of water, 1/8 cup of flour and ¼ cup of confectionary
sugar and mix until it becomes like a dough

Flour an area on your counter or cutting board and roll out the dough
Pour ½ cup of confectionary sugar and spread out until smooth.
Then add ¾ cup of something sweet like caramel, peanut butter,
honey etc. spread out and cover with another ½ cup of confectionary
sugar. Spread it out smooth. Now roll the dough up into a log.
Sprinkle the top with confectionary sugar and cinnamon. Chill for at
least a hour. Then you can cut it into 1 inch size pieces and serve.

Dough rolled and ready to chill

Bad Ass Vegan Fish Sandwich

BAD ASS VEGAN FISH SANDWICH
(recipe and photos courtesy of CleanFoodDirtyGirl.com)

INGREDIENTS:

1 package firm or extra firm tofu
½ cup cornmeal
½ cup whole wheat flour
1 tabs. dried basil, 1 tabs. garlic powder, 1 tabs. onion powder, 2
tabs. dulse flakes, t tabs. sea salt, 10 turns fresh black pepper, ¼ cup
unsweetened non-dairy milk, 1 cup high heat oil for frying.

PREPARATION:

Drain and rinse the tofu and set aside in a colander to drain.
(to make it drain even better, place a plate on top of the tofu and set
something heavy on it, set aside for now)
Make the breading by placing the cornmeal, flour, spices into a
mixing bowl. Whisk to combine and set aside

Take tofu and set it on a cutting board. Cut in hald and then in quarters. Take each of the quarters and slice them into thin pieces. You should be able to get 7-8 slices out of one of the quarters. Now heat your oil in a skillet on medium low.

Place the non-dairy milk in a small bowl. Take each piece of tofu and dip it in the non-dairy milk and then dredge it in the breading, making sure to coat the tofu well on all sides.
Place on a large plate and repeat until all of the tofu is covered in breading. When the oil is hot and starting to splatter, add as much tofu as you can fit in the skillet.
Cook for 3 minutes or until golden brown on one side. Flip over and cook until golden brown.
Take the tofu out of the pan and place on a brown paper bag so the oil gets soaked up by the bag.
Repeat with the rest of the tofu until all has been fried.
Allow to cool and serve with vegan tartar sauce, or make it into a sandwich.

TARTAR SAUCE:

Mix in a bowl until well combined:

½ cup vegan mayo
¼ cup sweet pickle relish, ½ tsp. lemon juice
½ tsp. sugar, 5 turns fresh black pepper.

Bad Ass Vegan Fish Sandwich

Cauliflower Scampi

CAULIFLOWER SCAMPI:
(Edward J Asprinio-Eddy Guitar)

In a large pot add 3 cups of olive oil, 2 cloves of garlic (diced) and ½ tsp. crushed red pepper. Simmer at low hear for 5 minutes. Add 2 heads of cauliflower that you have chopped up, and cook gently until Cauliflower is tender. Drain off oil in a colander.
Add salt and pepper to taste.
Cook 1 ½ pounds of pasta according to directions.
Drain water from pasta and add cauliflower mixture.
Add Parmesan cheese as desired

Pasta Fagioli

PASTA FAGIOLI :
(Joyce Landi)

In a large pot add:
1 gallon of water, 1 whole onion, a pinch of crushed red pepper,
2 tablespoons of salt, 2 celery stalks (leaves included) and 2
teaspoons tomato paste and garlic powder to taste.

Simmer in a covered pot for approximately 60 minutes.
Remove the onion and celery

Drain the liquid from 2 cans of kidney beans, add one can and mash
up the beans in the other can. Add to soup mixture.
Add ½ box of pasta.
Cook until pasta is tender. Turn off the heat and let it stand for 10-20
minutes to allow the soup to thicken.
Enjoy!

CHAPTER TWENTY-SEVEN: LISA'S BEAUTY RECIPES

CARROT FACIAL/FOR OILY TO NORMAL SKIN

Cook 2-3 large carrots and mash well, cook and add:
Add 4 ½ tsps. honey
Mix together
Put on your skin and leave on for ten minutes
Wash off

APPLE MASK/ FOR OILY SKIN ACNE PRONE

Grate one medium sized apple and mix with 5 tab. Honey
Mix and leave on your skin for ten minutes. Wash off

CLEAN FOOT RECIPE
Mix ½ cup water and ½ cup lemon juice in a bowl
Dip paper towels in the mixture and rub on feet
This removes odors

STRAWBERRY FOOT EXFOLIANT
8 strawberries
2 tab. olive oil
1 tsp. kosher salt
mash it into a paste, do not over blend
massage into feet and rinse

HAND EXFOLIANT

2 tab. oil, 3 tbs. sugar
make into a paste
rub into hands and rinse

DRY HANDS

1 tab. lemon juice
1 tsp. sugar
a bit of water
mix and rub onto hands and rinse

DEEP CONDITIONER FOR HAIR

1 small jar of real mayo
½ of a avocado
squish with hands until minty green
put in hair and wrap with saran wrap
leave on for 20 minutes
wash hair as usual

or you can use this mixture:
1 tsp. baby oil
1 egg yolk, 1 cup water
beat and mix well
massage into hair. Leave on 20 minutes rinse out

EYES
To sooth eyes place cucumber slices on closed eyes
And relax for half hour

For dark circles or bags under the eyes
Put warm tea bags on closed eyes for 10-15 minutes

HONEY CLEANSING SCRUB
Mix 1 tab. Honey
2 tbs. finely ground almonds
½ tsp lemon juice
mix and put on your face
wait ten minutes and rinse

FIRMING FACE MASK

1 tab. honey
1 egg white
1 tsp. glycerine
make a paste and leave on face ten minutes
rinse off

MOISTURE MASK FOR FACE

2 tab. honey
2 tsp. milk
mix and leave on face for ten minutes
rinse

SKIN LOTION
1 tsp. honey
1 tsp. vegetable oil
¼ lemon
mix and leave on face for ten minutes (or any part of your body)

AVOCADO MOISTURIZER

Peel avocado and rub on your face
Leave on for 15 minutes
Rinse

AVOCADO FACIAL CLEANSER

Beat 1 egg yolk
Add ½ cup milk
And ½ avocado mashed
Mix or use a blender
Use cotton balls to apply
Refrigerate to keep good for a few days

HAND TREATMENT

In a small bowl mix:
¼ avocado
1 egg white
2 tsp. oatmeal
1 tsp. lemon juice
apply to hands and leave on 20 minutes

PUFFY EYE TREATMENT

Peel avocado and remove the pit
Slice a half into ¼ inch crescents
Lie down and place under each eye
Rest for 20 minutes

DRY SKIN MASK
Beat 1 egg yolk
And ½ of an avocado mashed
Leave on 20 minutes

OILY SKIN MASK

1 egg white
1 tsp. lemon juice
mash ¼ of a avocado
blend in blender
leave on 20 minutes

or this is good too:

in a blender put
½ peeled cucumber
1 tab. yogurt
put on face for 20 minutes

or mash a few strawberries and add 1 tsp. honey
apply to face for 15 minutes

TO LOOSEN BLACKHEADS
Mix equal parts baking soda and water
Rub gently on skin 2-3 minutes
Rinse

OATS WITH HONEY SCRUB
½ cup uncooked oatmeal
1 tab. honey
1 tab. cider vinegar
1 tsp. ground almonds
blend into a thick paste
apply to moistened skin
allow to dry
remove with water and a wet face cloth

LEMON TONER
½ cup lemon juice, 1 cup distilled water
2/3 cup witch hazel. Combine and put in a bottle and store in refrig.
Pat on skin when needed

ACNE TREATMENT

2-3 tsp. dried basil
1 cup boiling water
steep basil for 10-20 minutes
allow to cool
apply with cotton balls

OILY SKIN TREATMENT

½ cup cooked oatmeal
1 egg white, 1 tab. lemon juice
½ cup mashed apple
beat into a paste
apply for 15 minutes and rinse

FACIAL SCRUB SOAP

Ingredients:
Glycerine
Oatmeal
Wheat germ
Sea salt

Melt glycerine
Boil one pan of water
Then add oatmeal, wheat germ sea salt.
Mix with glycerine and mix
Pour into molds.
Cool

TO REDUCE REDNESS OF A BLEMISH

Cut a slice of potato and apply like a compress

CHAPTER TWENTY-EIGHT: MILK, CHEESE, BUTTER AND EGGS

All the recipes in this book that call for milk, butter, or cream cheese are just common words that we use all the time. What we prefer to use in the recipes are animal friendly substitutions. As we know, dairy is one of the cruelest part of the animal industry. The cows are kept pregnant so they produce milk, the babies are taken away at birth and either kept for new dairy milk cows or sent to the slaughter house. Baby cows are used for veal and the stomach lining is used to make cheese.

For example: instead of milk you can use: soy milk, almond milk, or coconut milk. these are all good products, just find the brands you like the best.

As for cheese, there are many vegan cheese products on the market now you can buy. The same for whipped cream, we can use cool whip instead.

or butter, try "I can't believe it's not butter, or "good earth brands"

or use oleo.

Try these for baking with without eggs:
2 heaped Tabs. potato starch equals 1 egg
1/3 cup applesauce equals 1 egg
1/4 cup soy yogurt equals 1 egg
1 Tabs. ground flax seed and 3 Tabs. water equals 1 egg
1/2 banana pureed (or 1/4 cup) equals 1 egg
1/4 cup vegetable oil equals 1 egg
2 heaped Tabs. arrowroot powder equals 1 egg
1 Tabs. soy flour and 2 Tabs water equals 1 egg

Milk, cheese, and butter are some of the top three foods many people have a hard time giving up when switching to a healthy,plant-based diet. Even though the plant-based milk industry is now booming, thanks to all the varieties of options that we have, many people still do use dairy milk, cheese, and butter. But is this a coincidence? Is cheese pizza really something magical or is it addictive for so many people because of something else?

The reason why they're so addicting is largely due to a certain type of protein dairy products which is casein and whey protein. Thirty-eight percent of the solid matter in milk is made of protein. Of that total protein, 80 percent is casein and 20 percent is whey. Cheese is made mostly of casein, where most of the liquid whey found in milk has been filtered or strained out. But all dairy products contain casein, not just cheese. The difference between whey and casein is how they're digested and how they react in the body. Whey protein is digested quickly and absorbed rapidly into the bloodstream, which causes an increase in insulin quickly. This process stimulates IGF-1 (insulin growth factor which has been found to create new cancer cells and proliferate cancer cell growth. Casein is very different from whey, though just as detrimental to your health. Casein breaks down more slowly and in the process, also wreaks havoc on your health. Dr. T. Colin Campbell, author of The China Study, he has found casein to be the most relevant cancer promoter ever discovered. Because casein digests so slowly, natural morphine-like substances in casein known as Casomorphins act like opiates in the body as they enter the bloodstream. Just minutes after you eat a dairy-based food, the casein protein begins to break down. This releases the drug-like casomorphins, which attach to opiate receptors in the brain, and cause severe addictions to dairy products. Casomorphins trigger such an addictive response that they've been compared to heroine in terms of their strength to cause food addictions and mood disorders. Casein's slow digestion rate also puts great strain on the digestive system. Dr. Frank Lipman (an Integrative and Functional Medical expert), explains that the body has an difficult time breaking down casein. Dr. Lipman says that common symptoms of dairy sensitivity due to casein are: excess mucus production, respiratory problems and digestive problems like constipation, gas, bloating, and/or diarrhea. Dairy intolerance is also known to cause skin issues like acne, and rashes. If you still think a harmless glass of milk, a cup of yogurt, or a small serving of cheese isn't potentially dangerous, think again. Dr. Neal Barnard,M.D. (founder of the Physician's Committee for Responsible Medicine, a.k.a PCRM) found that in various studies, when dairy products were removed from the diet, cheese was the hardest food for people to give up. Dr. Barnard credits this finding to cheese being the most concentrated source of casein of all dairy products. PCRM has also discovered that milk actually contains morphine, which can clearly be seen when milk is inspected under a microscope. Morphine is not added to cow's milk; cows actually produce these opiate-like chemicals on their own.

The trouble with Casein is that it's not just found in dairy products. In fact, this dangerous ingredient is often used in other foods, even those that are marketed as a vegan food. Casein is used in food for its scientific properties to thicken and congeal foods and likely for its addictive properties to sell more products. Some brands of veggie cheeses, non-dairy yogurts, non-dairy, and non-dairy creamers contain casein for these very reasons. Casein is also found in some other non-food items such as: paint, adhesives, glues, fabrics, textiles, and plastics. You'll find casein listed as either of the following: casein, caseinates, calcium caseinate, potassium caseinate and sodium caseinate. Read labels thoroughly and buy products that are 100 percent vegan to be sure you're not consuming this ingredient, Lactose, a milk sugar found in dairy is also one of the number one allergies people have in the United States. Plant-based foods come with just as many satisfying properties as dairy foods do, yet they contain no morphine or other nasty chemicals found in dairy foods.

You can get lots of recipes at this website: onegreenplanet .org they also have a newsletter you can sign up for.

CHAPTER TWENTY-NINE: FINAL THOUGHTS

Thank you for taking the time to read this amazing cookbook and I hope you keep it close by and take advantage of the great recipes. Did you know that many kinds of high protein meat substitutes are available at your local markets? Including chicken, ham, and bologna style lunch meats, veggie burgers and hot dogs? Try them, you might find some you will really like. Some brands you will like better then others.

Eating less meat can be as easy as substituting a marinara sauce for a meat sauce, or a bean burrito instead of one with meat.

And all dining establishments offer many foods that do not contain meat.

So by reducing the amount of meats we eat can lessen the harm to animals.

You could make one or two days a week meat free, or one meal per day meat free. It will still help a great deal.

If you would like some more information on how you can help Vegan Outreach offers a free starter guide.

you can write to them with your request at: P.O. Box 30865 Tucson Az. 85751-0865

And if you check out the website you can get more information on helping animals and the environment by eating less meat and dairy products.

"We are deeply disassociated from so much of the animal cruelty in our society," This conduct would not be tolerated if it were visible."
Wayne Pacelle, the president of the Humane Society of the United States"

What kind of mindset are we really in, when we can look at a living creature and say to ourselves, I am going to eat you.

And don't forget karma:
Someday something might think, your tasty and crunchy!

A STORY

The Creature said to the man, "Oh, I think I will have you for dinner."

The man, who has the gift of speech replied, "But why? give me a good reason to kill and eat me."

The Creature said to the man, "Because, you are tasty."

The man said, "But that is not a good enough reason to kill me and take away my life."

The Creature replied to the man, "Well then, I have to feed my family."

The man said, "But that is still not a good enough reason either, meat is expensive and there are so many other things you can feed to your family."

The Creature said, " Well then, I have a recipe that calls for meat and I need meat to make it."

The man said, " That is still not good enough, you can make a different recipe, or make it without meat, or use something else instead of the meat. I am sure you are smart enough to figure it out." The Creature replied back, " Well, I don't care, your tasty and I want meat!" Well, logic did not work, and the man became the Creature's meal.

Then the Creatures started to factory farm man. They built huge buildings where they could breed large quantities man, faster and faster to feed the masses. Soon man never saw the light of day, had no family or any sort of social life. One day the Creatures invented fertility drugs, so they could produce more of man. They also invented drugs to keep man from getting sick in overcrowded conditions. They also invented hormones to make man grow faster and bigger. And baby man was most tender, and desired by many for special dishes. Man was fed a diet of vegetables and grain and also the waste parts of man. Nothing was wasted in the production of man, for high profits meant everything to the Creatures. (they even made "mandogs," and we don't even want to know what goes into them!)

This was all well for the Creatures as they got rich, had lots of food and were happy. Man was not.

Some Creatures rebelled against this unnatural way of keeping man and using him and his offspring for food. They rebelled against the way they were brought up, being taught to eat Man. Logically they did not understand why the other Creatures would want to eat something that is dead. This society of Creatures, have always had a custom of burying the dead, so this did not make sense to them. So these rebellious Creatures started to live by only eating the vegetables and fruits of their planet. Over time these Creatures became more healthy, and shiny and colorful. They did not know why, but enjoyed their new healthy lives without eating Man. Then one day far into the future, Man became toxic without the Creatures knowing it. And one day, all the Man eating Creatures died, all of them, all at once!

Then Man was free, they left the factory farms with the help of the Creatures that refused to eat Man. They built new lives and raised families. Practically overnight, this Planet became one of peace, Creatures and Man living together.

Being kind and loving each other, Creature and Man, Man and Creature. The End.

When I was a child one of the books I read was about Albert Schweitzer. I was amazed of what a wonderful person he was. I always looked up to him. He impressed me as being a great man.

And I came across a quote of him while writing this book.

"Until we extend our circle of compassion to all living beings, Humanity will not find peace, Albert Schweitzer."

So do your best, here are some ideas:

Be a Breakfast Vegetarian, this is easy, you can have anything for breakfast, just don't add meat. Or how about oatmeal with fruit, eggs with a English muffin, Morning Star or any non-meat sausage brand with eggs or on toast.
This is a good first step to help you on your way. And don't forget it's important to have something to eat in the morning.

After you conquer this you can move on to being a Breakfast and Lunch Vegetarian. Or how about a Weekend Vegetarian? It all works and makes a difference. There are lots of good healthy foods you can have for lunch without adding meat. A bean burritos, a nice big salad, grilled cheese and soup, all kinds of wraps and sandwiches and if your eating out, so many choices without meat. And when I am out and they have a great sounding dish, that contains meat, just request it without the meat.
So, good luck and thanks for trying. Its a big step to make but well worth the effort.

And don't forget this is all for the animals!
I left lots of space in this cookbook, so you can write in your own thoughts and recipes

The opinions and thoughts that I have written in this book do not necessarily reflect the opinions of my family and friends who have donated recipes for this book.
In the end, we all make our own choices.
And I could blab on and on, and tell you all kinds of logic, reasons, show you pictures of the cruelty, explain animal rights, morality, compassion, environmental concerns of factory farming, but at "The End" of this book, it does not matter how much knowledge you might have in your head, it has to reach your heart. Only then will it be possible to change.

Duck and Spider

Written and Illustrated
by
Barbara Nagle

SECRET FRIENDS

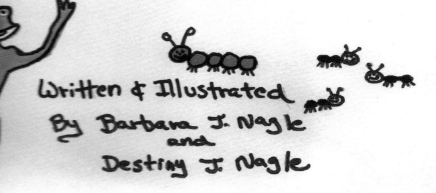

Written & Illustrated
By Barbara J. Nagle
and
Destiny J. Nagle

TABITHA

A TRUE STORY BY BARBARA J. NAGLE

The Tabitha Tree

by Barbara J. Nagle

This is a DVD well worth buying. It's a moving amazing story of
Farmer's who have found in themselves the compassion to change their outlook
on farming animals.

Peaceable Kingdom: The Journey Home

Harold Brown (Actor), Cheri Ezell-Vandersluis (Actor), Jenny Stein
(Director) Rated: Unrated Format: DVD

I would love to hear what you thought of
this Dvd and this cookbook.
Please contact me at: zling13@comcast.net

Change The World Cookbook by Barbara J. Nagle

First Printing 2015

All recipes in this book have been freely donated.

Cover artwork donated by Michael Murray, a most talented creative
artist. He is available for freelance work.(please contact the author if
you would like to contact Michael for any art projects)

Author: Barbara J. Nagle (middle) and daughter, Lisa Jean learning techniques from "The Notorious Cook", Jacqueline Sewell.

EATING MEAT IS A PERSONAL CHOICE?
YOU'RE FORGETTING SOMEONE.